The Stories
We Tell

The Stories We Tell

JOANNA GAINES

MAGNOLIA
PUBLICATIONS

Harper Select

Published by Harper Select, an imprint of HarperCollins Focus LLC.

Any internet addresses, phone numbers, or company or product information printed in this book are offered as a resource and are not intended in any way to be or to imply an endorsement by Harper Select, nor does Harper Select vouch for the existence, content, or services of these sites, phone numbers, companies, or products beyond the life of this book.

The information on page 216 is from Carol Graham and Julia Ruiz Pozuelo, "Happiness, Stress, and Age: How the U-Curve Varies Across People and Places," *Journal of Population Economics* 30 (2017): 225–264.

ISBN 978-1-4003-3387-5 (HC)
ISBN 978-1-4003-3388-2 (Ebook)
ISBN 978-1-4003-3389-9 (Audio)

Library of Congress Cataloging-in-Publication Data on File

Printed in the United States of America

22 23 24 25 26   LSC   10 9 8 7 6 5 4 3 2 1

To my kids,
Dauke, Ella, Duke, Emmie Kay & Crew:

May you always see
the beauty in every piece
of your story. ♥

Contents

CHAPTER ONE

A Story
to Tell

The first book I wrote, no one will ever read. I was a senior in college and a broadcast journalism major, so it wasn't entirely unusual that I would take up a writing project. But this book wasn't meant for the masses. It was just for me, and just for that season.

It was the summer of 2000, and I'd lined up a pretty decent internship at CBS News in New York City. It was my first time living away from home, and in addition to being a nervous wreck, I was realizing quickly that the world of television news wasn't for me. Most days, I'd leave my internship feeling uncertain or just plain homesick. I couldn't make sense of what I wanted for my future, yet as I walked those big city streets, I came upon parts of myself I hadn't been looking for.

I grew up in Rose Hill, Kansas, a small town outside Wichita. As a little girl who happened to be half-Korean, shy, and a little bit self-conscious, I was teased in the same ways a lot of kids get teased at school. There were certain parts of me that anyone could see, parts of my story you could glean from the surface of my skin. I looked different from all the other kids, for one thing. I tried my best to fit in, acting as though I didn't get their jokes about my slanted eyes or hear their whispers when I'd opt for rice instead of fries in the cafeteria line. I learned quickly that there were parts of me that could draw attention I wasn't interested in. But that was only at school. At home, I was the proud daughter of a beautiful Korean woman.

Here's the short version of a very complicated yet beautiful love story: My mom met my dad in Korea in 1971. He'd been drafted in the lottery to serve in the Vietnam War in '69. My dad was stationed in Seoul when he met my mother at a party one weekend. They fell in love, and when my dad returned to the States, they wrote letters back and forth, both of them having to use a translator to understand the other's written language. A year later, my father mailed my mom a plane ticket with a note attached that said: "Will you marry me? If you say no, will you at least mail the ticket back?"

A few months later, my mom landed in San Francisco, California, where she married my dad at the justice of the peace. She didn't know any English or anyone else. She was nineteen.

She figured out quickly how to conform to the culture in Kansas. My dad always talks about how fiercely mom worked to learn the culture and the language. She picked up some American ways of living—how other women dressed and interacted, as well as their mannerisms.

There were not a lot of other mixed-race families in Rose Hill that resembled ours, so it wasn't easy for my mom to feel like she could fit in. Years later, it wasn't easy for me either. I can look back now and see how my mom shaped the life of our family in ways that were unique to her culture—but then, my sisters and I didn't know the difference between a Korean tradition and an American one. We were both, and they were the same. To my sisters and me, our mom seemed as American as all the other kids' moms. We adored her the way little girls do. I loved her hair and the way she dressed. I was proud to be her daughter. I never thought of her as different. I didn't even realize that she spoke with an accent until a kid in my class pointed it out to me.

My mom had been helping in my classroom one afternoon when a boy who I'd grown used to making fun of me started to laugh and point, and announced, "No one can understand your mom when she talks." At first I thought, *What is he talking about? My mom's voice is normal.* It didn't even make sense to me.

Still, I felt a sting of shame rise up, but I didn't fully understand why, so I pushed it back down as quickly as it came and carried on, believing I didn't notice the differences between us—and really not noticing that my own beginnings of insecurity were part of the reason I didn't.

That same year, my mom's mother left Seoul to come live with us in Kansas. The first time I met her I thought she was so different from my mom. I didn't know what a traditional Korean grandmother was supposed to be like, but mine didn't wear makeup or color her hair—I could tell from all the streaks of gray. She wore really simple clothes while my mom was always dressed to the nines. And during the many years she lived with us, she only ever spoke Korean.

As different as they looked to me on the outside, I would learn to see that my mom and grandmother shared a past that ran deeper than anything. The history and heritage between them linked their hearts to a world I'd never known.

They went everywhere together. They'd drop my sisters and me off at school together, help in my classroom together, show up at my track meets side by side. It seemed like the more the other kids saw my grandmother with me, the more convinced they became of how different I was. And being different meant getting called names. It meant eating alone. I grew up thinking I had two options: fit in or be called out. So I dressed the way the other girls dressed. I laughed off insults. I told the other kids my middle name was Ann because it sounded more American than Lea (pronounced Lee). The lies I told out loud, though, weren't as harmful as the lies I was letting take root in my heart—that the person I was made to be wasn't good enough, that I'd have to learn to push aside the part of my family's history that didn't seem like it fit into the corner of the world I lived in.

As I got older, I watched it play out with my mom as well, in how she pretended not to notice the slow glances at the grocery store or hear the quiet insults under someone's breath. So I pretended too.

Eventually, the lunchroom teasing stopped. But by then I'd spent nearly twelve years quieting half of who I was in a world I thought wouldn't accept it, that somewhat subconsciously I'd forgotten it was ever a part of me to begin with. It wasn't until those lonely weekends in New York that I felt a nagging sense that those lost parts of me were ready to be found.

MANHATTAN IS A BEAUTIFUL MOSAIC of diverse races, personalities, and cultures. I stepped into that city as a twenty-one-year-old, and I'd never seen so many people who looked like me. I spent many weekends in Koreatown, as much for the sights and tastes and faces that reminded me of my mom and my grandmother as for my growing interest in the rich culture I found packed into just a few blocks in the heart of Midtown. At first, it was our sameness that comforted me in a place that felt so big and foreign, but then it was the way they lived in the fullness of their culture that drew me back. The streets bustled with Asians of all backgrounds, and I couldn't help but see my own reflection in the young girls who passed by, hand in hand with their mothers. Finally, I was seeing the beauty of being different and the thrill of being unique. For the first time in maybe forever, I was proud of who I was, and I was realizing that the part of me that *is* different and *is* unique really is the most beautiful part of my story.

I decided to get it all down on paper—the chapters of my life I'd shelved and let collect dust for too long. At night, I'd come home from my internship and I would write and write—*everything*. As quickly as my pen could keep pace with my heart, trailing its way across the page. I started with the earliest memory I could recall, all the way back to elementary school, detailing the moments I'd tried so hard to forget— the small, yet significant characteristics of each one—to see if I could get close enough to feel them. All the teasing and all the lies I'd let take root in my heart, I crossed out and rewrote with truth. Before long, I was weeping for that little girl, for how long she'd gone through life believing that who she was wasn't enough.

But this is what I learned during those painful nights: the only way to break free was to rewrite my story. Because something would happen every time my pen stopped, night after night. It was like my soul was coming back to my body. Like the deepest parts of me that got knocked around and drowned out by all the crap I let the world convince me about who I was came back to the surface. And what was left was only what was real and true.

As I sat there, with years of living and learning behind me, I wanted so badly to go back in time and tell that little girl that not only is she good enough—she is extraordinary.

I didn't think that writing down my story would heal me, but it did. Whatever hurt I came to New York carrying, I could feel it start to untangle itself free.

You likely have parts of your own history you'd rather forget, same as I do. But when I actually wrote these things down, when I got up close and personal with them—yes, there was pain, and yes, there was hurt—by giving them a name, I stripped them of their power. And what I learned is that lies will always be worth fighting against. Because what you're left fighting *for* is the truth, and that is the most freeing thing in the world.

Once I knew, deep in my soul, how it could feel to live out the truth of who I was, I got a taste for a new kind of meaning in life. Meaning that makes living any other way feel like wasted time. All the untrue memories that came before felt like meaningless scenes stitched together, and those moments lost their color. And you don't want to go back to being normal; you want to go back even further. Back before the world got its hands on you. Before other people got their hands on you. And you crave that perspective again and again and again.

SO HERE I AM, a couple of decades later, longing once again to write everything down. A few of the same things that drew me to my journal and pen at the age of twenty-one have brought me back: a yearning for healing, for clarity, for steadiness. The end of last year brought this desire into focus.

Things had gotten blurry. *I'd* gotten blurry. My forty-fourth birthday was just around the corner, and I was realizing, for the first time, that it meant I was nearly halfway through this life of mine. I looked around at what I'd built with equal parts gratitude and exhaustion. I love my life, and I love my family—deeply. But some of the ways I'd gotten here, some of the qualities I'd always relied on—like being really productive, superefficient, always running at high capacity—were beginning to turn on me. The last twenty years have been a heck of a ride, but I knew I couldn't keep going the way I have. My adrenaline was slowing, revealing in its absence insecurities and unhealthy habits from way back when that I'd been moving too fast to deal with.

It's hard to explain how I was feeling. I was grateful beyond measure, but exhausted. Loved, but feeling unworthy. Full, but running on empty. I started to experience anxiety for the first time in my life. It was taking me longer to be inspired but less time to become tired. And because my world kept me busy, I could still feel the wheels of my life humming. What became harder to tell is where they were headed.

I could also sense that I was nearing a bend in the road. My oldest son was touring colleges at the same time I was touring preschools for my youngest. Lately, life had felt like a twisted game of tug-of-war—not knowing what I should let go of and what I should hold tight to. My little corner of the world was turning, quickly, and I feared I'd miss it completely if I didn't start living differently.

For a time, I figured the fix had something to do with my schedule or a lack of something—focus, inspiration maybe? So I made space in my calendar to nurture things that filled me up. I took more days off, and I made more meals at home. I got a few facials, took a few naps. I decluttered closets and put away my phone more often. These things helped move the needle, but it wasn't the turnover I was looking for.

I needed to figure out what, about the way I'd been living, was wearing me out. I was ready to catch my breath and look closely at my life. To retrace as many moments of pain and regret and grief as there have been moments of beauty and grace and joy. To slow down enough to celebrate the wins and learn from the losses. To navigate all that I'm carrying here and now—noting what needs to be left behind so I can move forward a little lighter, a little freer. To learn what was holding me back and what would inch me closer to the kind of life I was building in my dreams.

So I started to write—again. This time also combing through years of journal entries. I had, spread out before me, a mighty collection of memories and moments and prayers upon prayers. Lots of wishful thinking and plenty of hang-ups. Pain I was trying to forget among dreams I didn't want to. Journaling is something I've tried to do every day for I don't know how long. It's always been a reliable way for me to work things out. I'm an introverted type, and sometimes talking in a group only makes things cloudier in my brain. Writing is how I can make sense of things—problems, ideas, the world, and my place in it. My journal is where I talk to myself and to God. It seems like I don't really know how I feel about something until I've written it down. Sussed it out. Until I've given my thoughts a chance to arrange themselves in a more purposeful way.

After a while, I could sense that I was writing *toward* something. What, exactly, I wasn't sure. But there, among the scribbles and notes and my heart poured out, it was starting to read like a story—like my story.

Sure, there were some random thoughts, some ramblings and lists and wishes, but in between the marks of to-dos was the whole of my life, written in my hand.

It was messy and winding and beautiful, and graciously revealed about a million wonders. Some of it broke my heart—and some of it pieced it back together. But every part, every note, every memory was woven into whatever came next—and it all felt so well-played. No matter how shameful or embarrassing, how happy or joyful, each chapter was the bridge that led me to the next place I was meant to go.

The truth I'd been missing was right there on those pages: my life *is* a story. A *good* one. And for as many moments I've lived that brought me to my knees, more moments have made my soul sing.

The other truth? I wouldn't have to change my life completely. I only needed to learn how to hold it all differently. I *can* feel gratitude and slow down long enough to savor it. I *can* be loved and find myself worthy of it. I *can* feel full and not just in glimpses, but in long-lasting ways that satisfy the life I'm craving.

It started with that picture you see on the cover of this book. Because that little girl, the one with the missing tooth and messy hair— she knew who she was before the world chimed in. And part of writing down my story has been in hopes of finding her again.

It felt like a rescue mission. For that, I told no one about this writing project except Chip and a couple of close friends. It was too personal, too vulnerable, too unpolished to know if it was meant to mean something to anyone but me. I wanted to keep this idea close to my chest until I was sure about how and when I wanted to share it. *If* I'd ever want to.

My heart changed about halfway through writing down my story. It could have been because I started with all the painful, hard stuff first. Stories that brought shame and my soul's deepest insecurities to the page. Past hurt resurfaced and so did pain I've prayed to forget. And yet, slowly—emphasis on *slow*—I was starting to feel healing in places I'd felt broken. I was beginning to have some clarity in areas that had felt cloudy for years. I was, finally, standing in the fullness of my story. I felt hopeful. I felt full.

Our story may crack us open, but it also pieces us back together.

I'M GOING TO try to persuade you to recognize the power of knowing your story and owning it in every way, because, like mine, your story is yours alone. It's one of a kind. It seems to me that there are very few absolutes in this life; only a handful of things are true to their core. I believe your story is one of them, and there is infinite value in a life that seeks a meaningful story and is willing to be shaped by it.

Human beings have been telling stories as long as there's been a language to tell them in. For many thousands of years, since the first cave paintings, telling stories has been one of our most fundamental ways of communicating. And isn't almost every story a connection of cause and effect? The story of how you met your spouse. How you earned that scar. Why you're running late. Whether it's about buying groceries or a project at work, the story is what we remember. It's what we tell.

Stories also connect us. Without story, there is no history, no way of deeply knowing one another. A grandfather tells his life story to his children's children so years from now, that history will shape a new generation. I think about new hires at our company, and the importance of telling them stories about the early days at Magnolia, the foundation of those humble and hard-won beginnings, because that's what keeps the spirit of the company alive. We read stories to our children every night to teach them about the world and to free their imaginations. Stories don't ask for distance; they bring us in. We see ourselves in the characters, we resonate with the emotions, we recognize there are aspects of the human experience beyond what we've known.

So if we think in stories, remember in stories, speak in stories, and turn just about everything we experience into a story, what does that say about the value of your own?

The irony is that the first step in getting to know your story is getting out of your own way. Even in writing this book, my first obstacle was myself, believing the lie that if I was to share it, no one would want to hear what I have to say—blurring any good intention I had with questions about what makes me think my story is worth sharing. But once I flipped that script and changed my mindset to the truth—that I have an amazing story to tell—I was freed. Because if there's even just one single person who hears pieces of my life and it helps them in their own journey, it will have been worth it. And then when you hear how

profound and influential sharing your story can be—the connection
it can create—it seems almost selfish to keep our own buried inside.

MY JOURNEY SINCE New York has only strengthened my notion
of story. When Chip and I were just getting our construction and home
renovation business off the ground, I didn't know a lot about the art of
home design. I hadn't gone to school to learn the best industry practices
for interior spaces, but I knew how it felt to be held by a home. I had an
instinct for creating spaces that said something about the people who
lived there. Spaces that supported who they were and honored the story
of their home and their family. I've said it before, but I truly believe
that a house becomes a home when it tells your story. When you can
approach the design of your home with intention, and you see something that has significance hanging on your wall or sitting on a shelf
you walk by daily, it's a reminder of where you've been and who you
are. Or maybe it represents something you want more of. I've come to
believe our homes can be filled with random, generic things or they can
convey some of our most important truths.

The same holds true for the story of our lives.

When *Fixer Upper* aired for the first time, Chip and I were
completely caught off guard by how people were responding to our story,
when to us it never felt any way other than ordinary—we were building
our lives around hard work that we loved to do. I don't think we'll ever
fully understand why people have resonated with our family the way

they have. I'm grateful it's happened, but these days I'm far more grateful for what it's shown us—that truth, vulnerability, and courage can make even the most everyday, ordinary life tell an extraordinary story. And I know for certain we are not the only ones living this way.

As our audience grew, so did our understanding of story. And not just the way it connects us to our truest selves and our most sacred spaces. It can also bridge strangers across state lines and stretch beyond language barriers. We've had opportunities to meet and work alongside people much different from us, opening our eyes to the breadth and diversity of the human experience. And ever since then, Chip and I have sort of become story-obsessed. We love to hear about people who are doing things they're passionate about—and it doesn't matter if that thing made a big splash or was forged in quiet, because even small courageous acts resound.

YOU CAN APPROACH telling your story any way you want. As I've shared, it's become a practice of mine to sit down and physically write these things on paper or in a journal. The act of writing—pen-and-paper style—brings in a whole other element. It isn't just words on a page. It requires intention. Every word carries a certain weight—and when strung together, a certain clarity. From my experience, this very deliberate expression brings us closer to how we truly feel. You get to see your inner thoughts appear in front of you—no middleman, no critique. You get to see that what bubbles up from within is worthy.

When you leave something of yourself somewhere tangible, it leaves a mark deeper than what you can see. Think about something handwritten that you've held on to—a love letter, a friend's encouragement, a worn-edged recipe card from your grandmother—and you can *feel* the power of putting pen to paper. You remember the way it felt to hold that promise in your hand. That's why much of my own story exists on paper. Lots and lots of paper, inside journals I keep piled on a shelf in my office.

When I say *story*, I don't mean history. The latter tends to take shape as a series of facts, and our brains aren't sparked by bullet points but context. The whole story. Any piece of our past and present that could use a little rebranding. For me, it's often the stuff that isn't easy to talk about—the things I bury, that I try to avoid reliving in my day-to-day. Yet I think it's there, right in the reliving, that we have the chance to change the narrative. Not letting a lie or misguided thought be the last thing we carry forward, but instead saving that space for the truth. And because I believe there is power in asking our body to act on our heart's behalf—even if we don't believe the truth *yet*—writing it down is a powerful first step. What you start to see is that the broken, the sad, and the hard, just as much as the fulfilled, the good, and the happy—all of it gets stitched together to make us whole.

Getting your story down needn't be in pursuit of happiness but rather wholeness. Not to feel perfect but more complete. To me, there's a grace woven into the very fabric of wholeness that invites us to live in the abundance of our story. Through that lens alone we can glean the clarity necessary to see ourselves as all that we are. But we can never be whole until we get up close and personal with every chapter of our lives. And when we interpret through the lens of time and maturity what we thought we saw or felt back then, that's usually when things start to look different. Hopefully, they get a little clearer.

Simply getting your story down might be transformative enough. I'm always looking for the invisible string that connects it all. When my pen stops, I want to have an idea of where I go from there. What did I learn, how have I changed? What do I carry forward, and more importantly, what do I need to leave behind?

I've learned to view my story as I'm writing it today as a blueprint for where I've been and where I'm at now, seeing how every chapter has woven together moments, both good and bad, that now shape who I am—my strengths, my interests, the gifts I carry. Without writing it down, without seeing that tapestry, we miss the perspective of knowing what's worth carrying forward, where we'll go next, and who we want to become when we get there.

AT TWENTY-ONE, I left New York believing that every bit of who I am and what I have to offer is mine to hold, to own, and to use to make beautiful things in this world. It's like I was seeing the full picture of my life for the first time, not just the highlight reel of rights and wrongs. I could see the way the good and the bad works together to make me uniquely who I am. The sum of it all became infinitely greater than each individual pain and each individual win. There was a sense of purpose there, hiding beneath all that stuff I'd been carrying around.

I realized how many years I had lived guarded. How long I'd shown up in pieces, only sharing the parts of me I felt confident in. The parts that people seemed to easily accept. But when I returned home from New York, I remember feeling *full*—resolved to move toward the fullness of who I am.

I DON'T THROW AROUND the word *purpose* lightly. I get that it can feel like a heavy notion. I know for me thoughts around "What is my life's purpose?" have often kept me up at night. Mostly because I worry that if I don't yet know, somehow I'm already behind—that I've already lost time. The idea of purpose also lacks tangibility—a "maybe, someday" revelation you cross your fingers hoping you'll stumble upon. But instead of choosing a mindset that makes it all too easy to live for tomorrow, what if the very things you're meant to breathe life into are closer than you think?

Take your story. What if finding purpose is a matter of reading between the lines? As you jot things down, look closely. What in life thrills you? What lies need to be cut from your daily perspective? To what ideas do your thoughts gravitate? Is there a deep-seated passion that's waiting to be brought to the surface? Then, it's simply a matter of bending your life toward that pursuit.

There is purpose to be found in the story you're living. But there's no direct path to being truly known if you don't allow yourself to be fully seen. No facades, no heightened portrayals. This kind of living requires vulnerability. It's uncomfortable to unearth the parts of your story that bring shame or embarrassment to the surface. But, what if a few moments of painful exposure save you from a lifetime of hiding in halfness? Would it be worth it then?

I think so.

That's why I'm sitting here, writing it all down again. You don't have to have it all figured out to join me. There are no walls here. I'm not trying to show you a side of me that's perfect and polished because it's in a book and I can edit it. Rather, I want you to meet me where I'm at in my story with where you're at in yours.

Perhaps you feel like you've already settled the score on past hurts and hang-ups, and you view both your history and your future through contented eyes. Maybe you walk through the present with a certain clarity about where life goes next.

But there's a good chance you haven't always felt so sure of things. Or you might not again somewhere down the road. And perhaps, when you sit here and think about it, you remember seasons when life felt like it simply *happened* to you. Maybe, like me, that's a feeling you resonate with today. You remember there being a graduation, a wedding, a delivery room. But the moments in between the milestones—that's where things get blurry.

I don't know about you, but when I look back, I don't want to see a kind of kaleidoscope life—out of focus and jumbled—where the moments I swore I'd never forget become difficult to discern amid the chaos of thoughts and memories unresolved. I want to live the next season of this beautiful life in focus, and in full pursuit of the life I'm called to.

Because this book is my story, and every chapter is a window into who I am, the journey I'm on, and the season I'm in right now, there are themes you'll see constantly—like vulnerability, fear, intentionality, perfectionism—that are unique to me. The chapters of your own life will be different. Maybe you won't always relate, or maybe it will feel like you're looking in a mirror. And like me, you might be at the halfway point of your life. Or perhaps you're way younger or way older. Whatever we have in common and whatever differences lie between us, I only hope my story can help shine a light on the beauty of yours. And that my own soul work will stir something of your own.

If you're feeling resistant, there's a good chance that you are your own first obstacle. At least that's how it usually works with me. Before you think, *I don't want to go there. Who cares about the past?* I'd argue that's pain and insecurity creeping in, trying to persuade you that it's not worth rewriting parts of who you've been so you can live in the fullness of all you truly are.

Also, though this book was written fairly quickly, I've been working through these things for a while. So I'm going to ask that you read this book slowly. Hopefully, at a pace that leaves room for your own story to unfold. Maybe journal after each chapter or go for a walk. Some chapters are heavy, some are light. But by the time you get to the end of my story, I hope you're holding the beautiful beginnings of your own.

A story only you can tell. And I hope that you will.

And just to be clear before we jump in, this book is not an autobiography. I'm not old enough, wise enough, or experienced enough to write an account of my life quite yet. I still have too much to learn and discover about myself, and I feel as though I am only halfway there. This book also is not a how-to, because I certainly don't have all the answers.

What I hope this book is for you is an invitation to come as you are. To join me, with a vulnerable and open heart, as we connect the chapters of our life stories and figure out where we go next, learning to move forward from within. Guard down, light shining. It's an invitation to a kind of life where you know how to hold what you believe—about yourself and the quiet worlds of the people you pass—with gracious and open hands. To see your story as greater than any past or future thing, but for all the beauty and joy and hope it holds today.

What do you say? What beautiful story is yours to tell?

I'll go first.

Our story may crack us open,

but it
also pieces
us back
together.

CHAPTER TWO

When Fear Breaks

Left to my own imagination, fear can have its way with me. A vivid memory came to mind a few weeks ago: me, as a little girl, maybe five or six, lying in my bed in the middle of the night. Frozen in fear. Wholly convinced, from the top of my head to the very tips of my toes, that a monster was hiding beneath me. I would lie there for what I remember feeling like hours, trying to problem solve. Thinking of solutions for how I could get through my door, to my parents' room, without it catching me. There wasn't ever an obvious escape route that didn't involve a serious risk of being face-to-face with this made-up monster, so I'd always resolve to stay as still as possible for as long as possible. Eventually I'd fall asleep, and when I woke up the next morning, it was always gone. I must have had it in my head that daylight was the only thing that could make it disappear, and darkness was what brought it back.

When you're young, fear is fear. It's harder to tell the difference between real, watch-out-for-that-car danger and the things we perceive to be equally frightening. And our young minds can't sort out reasoning well enough to ask where our fear is coming from, what is really simmering below the surface that might tell us something of why we're suddenly tingly all over, anxious, and desperately searching for somewhere to hide. We just know it when we feel it.

Then we get older and learn that fear that grows by night doesn't always dissolve by day. That actually, fear is everywhere. We can find it around every corner, every bend, if we're looking. Even when we're not, fear is skilled in the art of surprise.

I'M THE MIDDLE CHILD in my family, so I watched my older sister go off to kindergarten a few years before I could. When it was finally my turn, I was ready. Maybe it was the distraction of the thrill of it all, but somehow, I forgot that my new teacher had sent home a note saying that the first day would be a show-and-tell, where all the kids could bring in something to share with the class.

I forgot all about it until the first bell rang and my teacher started to call on my classmates. I didn't panic though—I had just the thing to show everyone. That morning, on the way to school, a button had fallen off my jacket. I'd slipped it into my coat pocket before I hopped out of the car. When my teacher called on me, I stood up and walked out into the hallway where all our coats hung on hooks. I think that walk was just long enough to build up some hype around what I might bring back inside with me. Quickly, I pulled the button from my coat pocket and closed my fingers tightly around it. I held my hands behind my back as I made my way to the front of the classroom, thinking to myself, *They're not going to believe this.*

I held out the button in the palm of my hand, with a look as if it glittered like gold. "This is my button," I said. "It fell off my jacket this morning on the way to school!" I waited for the *oohs* and *ahhs*, for heads to duck and reach to try and get a better look at the button I held in my hand. But the class stayed silent. So I froze too.

And then, one by one, laughter.

Even as I write about it now, I can still feel my blood rushing, my face flushed, as giggling bubbled up among the rows in front of me. My teacher, Ms. Primm, was the only one to hold my gaze; she had this look in her eyes that made me feel safe. Still, there I was thinking I'd nailed it in one second, and in the next, I was wishing I was anywhere but that classroom.

It all seems so innocent now, looking back on my first day of kindergarten. Me thinking a button would steal the show. All these years later, I'm laughing at myself too. And I get that in the grand scheme of moments that hurt us, of truly traumatic events, this one doesn't really stack up. But I don't think it was the moment itself that felt so defining. It was what it prompted, what came next, that still has me reeling. Because that day was the first time I can remember caring what people think. The first time I experienced insecurity, even if I couldn't have put that name to it, I felt it—that sting of rejection. It might have been a small moment, but I let it morph into a big lie. I let it breed a new kind of fear in me. One that told me I'd be wise to self-protect. And moments like that can still time, even in recollection. And somehow, they're more memorable when you didn't see them coming.

Fear was no longer a monster that stayed hidden beneath my bed. Because now I knew that fear could surprise me. There was a new world of unknowns now, where I feared any moment could catch me off guard as it had on that first day of school. I would go on to learn that fear can be cunning, that it was capable of weaving in and out of my days, moving and morphing into whatever I needed it to be to stay convinced that I kept myself guarded for good reason. That it's safer to stay put. That self-protection is essential. That I should continue to sharpen that instinct until it grows and festers and takes up residence deep in my heart.

In time, most of us grow out of the monster-under-the-bed phase. We learn that particular fear is make-believe, and we credit our imagination for having ever believed it to begin with. But I'm not so sure I ever really grew out of envisioning things that aren't there. Because as I got older, I was still imagining monsters everywhere.

I COULDN'T CATCH hold of fear, and I never knew what doors were safe to open, so I kept them all closed. As it turned out, fear was the one chasing me, turning up in all sorts of disguises. And even as I evolved, it could evolve too. Fear of the dark turned into fear of the unknown, and later, fear of failure. My first day of kindergarten taught me what it felt like to fear what people thought of me—their perceptions, mostly, but even more than that I think I learned to fear myself. How could I trust that I wouldn't be caught off guard like that again? The short answer is, I couldn't. No one can predict the human spirit.

My family moved around a lot for my dad's job. So those fears followed me to more classrooms and other first days. I can remember my first day of my sophomore year at a new high school. We'd just moved to Round Rock, Texas, which is about eighty miles south of Waco. I was the new girl in the biggest school I'd ever seen, entering a grade where most of the kids had been in one another's classes for a while. All morning, I was dreading lunch. Think back to your own high school cafeteria and you can probably understand why. Everyone sits with their group of friends, and if you don't belong to one, there's always that moment after you grab your lunch tray when you're searching the giant room for an open seat—or if we're being honest here, a pair of kind eyes inviting you to sit with them.

Everything about that scenario screamed at me to stay at a safe distance. As I stepped up to the tall double doors that welcomed me to the cafeteria, that old familiar fear washed over me, that monster that could always freeze me in place. Kids were pushing past me on either side, making the doors swing open every few seconds. From where I stood, it looked like chaos. Like a sea of people with not one open seat free for me. Not a single face I recognized. I wouldn't be able to walk through those doors for a couple of months, so every day I skipped lunch and hid in the library.

For years—too many years—I spent a great deal of energy avoiding walking through unknown doors. Fear deepened the ruts of my growing insecurities. Shame from being called out for being different in the lunchroom and trying to hide certain aspects of my story from a world I didn't think would accept them. Doubt about what I had to offer that people would be interested in.

So fear continued to trail me, masquerading as protection and safety. Promising me a life unscathed. Teaching me how to wear disguises of my own. Perfection, mostly, which is a word I use to soften the real desire, which is control. But here's what I've learned about perfection: it's isolating. And the more isolated I felt, the more fear grew.

Maybe perfection isn't your vice. Or even fear. But perhaps you do know what it's like to present yourself as you *want* to be seen rather than as you truly are. It might be to avoid looking weak, or too emotional. To avoid giving away the bumps and bruises you picked up on the way to where you are now. Or it could be pain from your past that keeps resurfacing, no matter how much you try to shade it in your shadow. And maybe, like me, you know how it feels to slowly fade back until you're all covered up, and the real you is so faint you're forced to look around, to other people and other things, for evidence of who you are.

I've been this turned around a few times in my life, and I've learned the hard way that fear, in its many forms, can make you feel invisible and powerless. Fear can derail your best intentions. It can keep you stuck in place no matter how badly you long to move forward. It can dictate where and why we show up in the world, the kind of story our lives tell, and how much of the real us we let people see—often without even noticing we've surrendered the truest parts of who we are.

I would come to learn that when we give fear that much power over our lives, we can never be sure we will get that power back. Because more often than not, fear isn't something you can grasp onto. It isn't something you can take and put in its rightful place. It's an illusion.

Those early days of high school got better. Eventually I found a few friends and a familiar table in the cafeteria, but that's not the point of the story. The point is that something kept me from walking through those doors sooner. In that moment, all signs pointed to fear. My hands shook, my breath shortened, my body froze. But as I look back at that moment, with a few decades of living and learning between us, I was wrong to give fear all the credit. Not when it was mostly make-believe. I was imagining something that was only half of the story. I told myself I was too afraid, but the truth is that I didn't know I could also be brave.

I couldn't have pieced it together then, but fear was the lie I told myself to avoid the part where we have to feel our way through all those ugly emotions we carry around with us—doubt, insecurity, pride. The part where we have to put one foot in front of the other, everything inside us screaming not to, just to make it through the door. No guarantees for what's waiting for us on the other side.

It can be a painful walk—that is why some of us will stay stuck in place, avoiding risk, uncertainty, or emotional exposure of any kind. Dodging arrows we think we see. Turning down a job for fear we'll be no good at it. Pushing down the words *I love you* for fear they won't be returned. Guarding our hearts from friends for fear they'll get too close and not like what they see. We call these things fear. We say we're too afraid. We freeze in place. And there it is again. That made-up monster we know we'll never catch.

I believe we all long to be brave. We all long for the courage to show up and be seen. Deep down we all crave a whole-hearted life. But then, a painful moment, a shaming comment, a false truth, and we're running for cover.

Fear rises. We break.

It took me a long time to flip that script. It wasn't until I was tired enough of living it—over and over again. Only when I felt completely worn down by fear and its control over my life did I start to ask myself what I was so afraid of to begin with. And only then could I see that what might have been a real threat at one point—a physical fear, a shame or insecurity, a moment of sincere pain—had since morphed and multiplied and spun out theories I let define me. And that wasn't the story I wanted my life to tell.

The reality is, we live in a vulnerable world. That much won't ever change. It's a world filled with pain and hurt and confusion. A world where unpredictable moments can cause us to want to guard our hearts, to steer clear of certain tendencies, to look out for ourselves, to blame our lack, or to prove the naysayers wrong. Some of us go on to define our lives in full pursuit of these defenses—even without noticing that we lose more of who we are every time we make ourselves small, every time we fail to remember we are more than those moments that hurt us.

But I would come to learn that vulnerability is also my path back. What knocks the wind out of me is what forces me to learn to breathe again. When my heart lays bare, when I step out of my shadow, uncovered and arms wide, and when I fail or fall, vulnerability is what picks me up, dusts me off, and carries me once more.

WHEN I MET CHIP, he didn't seem to have a fearful bone in his body. I envied his willingness to leap into unknowns while I kept fear close. The first year we were married, we were making decisions faster than I could process them. We were renovating our house and a couple of rental properties, and we'd started making improvements to a little building we'd bought to turn into a home and decor shop. Everything was risky because we had very little money and still a lot to learn. Our lives were already being fed on a steady diet of risk, failure, and growth. But things were moving too quickly for me to doubt, or to say no, which I likely would have if there'd been time. So we kept moving, kept renovating. The little shop, which we called Magnolia, was getting close to being ready to open, so my mom and I made a trip to Dallas to shop for inventory. When we showed up to the Dallas Market Center, there were twenty-five floors of wholesale vendors to walk through. Showroom after showroom. We spent the day there, and I remember staring at what felt like thousands of products wondering to myself, *Where do I even begin?* while the showroom rep looked at me with her pen and paper, asking again and again when I didn't answer, "Well, how many do you want?"

My world was finally slowing down long enough to trigger some of those familiar fears. Doubt, insecurity, shame—thinking I could pull off something like this. Opening Magnolia was by far the riskiest thing I'd ever done, so fear doubled down. I was questioning this big dream of mine—the first one I'd ever really had—but even more questioning whether I was the right person to bring it forth. I was doubting all the work we'd done and regretting all the money we'd spent, when, on the drive home, I started to get sick. My mom had to pull over the car, and something about that moment convinced me enough was enough.

Fear and I did a dance that day, right there in my mom's car on the side of the highway. I told myself I was capable, and I felt insecurity rise, then break. I told myself I could fail, but that it didn't have a hold on me, and I felt doubt rise, then break. I told myself this dream was worthy, and that I was too, and I felt all those years of fear and shame rise, then break.

Every decision after that day felt a little lighter, a little freer.

Not because I had rid myself of fear forever, but because I knew it was possible to rewrite that lie with truth. I couldn't have known how dangerous fear was until that moment—until I realized I actually felt safer in freedom's freefall. When I chose to believe in my inherent worth. And in this case, when I had people around who believed in it too. When I was willing to be vulnerable about how wildly I could fail. When I was willing to say, "I don't know what I'm doing, this won't be perfect, but I'm going to give it all I've got."

Everything about opening that little shop felt vulnerable. Magnolia was full of uncertainty and risk. I still worried people wouldn't like it, that they'd hate the products and this whole thing would be a big failure. But I would go through with it anyway. As I was learning with every wavering step I took, there was no way to chase a dream without being comfortable with failure. No way to deepen my well of creativity without sinking into uncertainty. No way of finding out if courage could ring louder than fear unless I tried. That's what living vulnerably was offering me. One, and then the other.

It was the only way I'd learn to confidently push aside the lie of fear so I could live and share my story in fullness and in truth. I can see how it may seem simpler—*safer*—to hang back, to avoid walking through unknown doors carrying all that stuff we work so hard to keep hidden. But it seems to me there's no use in pretending that any of us are safe from hurt, pain, or even disappointment. I'm starting to think we wouldn't want to be. Without hurt, we can never know trust. Without pain, we can never know what wholeness feels like—to love and to belong. And without disappointment, we can never know triumph.

I don't mean that we should put ourselves in danger, or that I don't believe fear keeps us safe to some degree. That biological siren that goes off in our heads when we need to quickly jump out of the way or slam on the brakes—that kind of fear is essential. It's only the kind of fear that starts to spin out make-believe scenarios that I've become weary of.

The day I opened the doors to Magnolia was the day I finally shut the doors on make-believe fear, forcing it to untangle its grip around my heart, to loosen its shackles around my ankles. That season bred a whole new dream for what my life could become. Imagine if I'd chosen not to open those doors. Too many dreams would have gone undreamed; too much in my life right now simply wouldn't exist.

Fear in general didn't disappear forever. I doubt it will. I'm not sure our lives will ever be void of that siren song that lures us to so-called safer ground. And I don't need mine to be.

I know how to find my way back now.

I MENTIONED HOW FAST Chip and I were running when we first got married. The thing is, we never really slowed down. In the first five years, we became parents four times over, and we were barely scraping by financially. I was fearing a whole lot of things: failure, our future, what people would think. I was exhausted by my own obsession with trying to hide our reality and keeping all the balls in the air. When I couldn't control our finances, I micromanaged our home and the kids. And because I couldn't fix the way I felt, I controlled the way our life looked. I couldn't get a handle on how to move forward, so I started to write it all down. At first, just for myself. And the more I wrote, the more fear broke. So I thought I'd start a blog, hoping there were other people out there who might resonate with me—like their life felt out of their control—but who also longed, more than anything, to carry their babies and their dreams not on their backs like burdens, but to hold them all dearly with grateful and gracious arms.

For someone who had learned to pride herself on being polished and put together, who only jumped when she could know for sure there was a safety net below, starting that blog felt like a raw and real expression of who I was, and that was a bit scary. But the more I wrote, and the more I shared, the more other people did too. It felt like the less I hid, the more willing I felt to be seen in a deeper way. Others too. Gradually, I became connected to this community of people who, amazingly, felt the same way I did. I couldn't believe so many other people were willing to bare their souls, in a way, from behind their own computers, in their own messy, chaotic, kid-filled homes.

Chip and I spent these same years buying and selling houses around Waco. I didn't go to interior design school, yet here we were leveraging our livelihoods on being able to flip homes. There was no degree of proof that I knew what I was doing. When *Fixer Upper* started filming our work, and people were actually watching us, this on-the-job skill I still had so much to learn about was suddenly center stage. People were calling me a designer. For a while, I felt like an imposter. Back then, it was just a job. A job we had so we could put food on the table. But Chip and I both loved the work, even when it came with a dozen cameras and even more reasons to second-guess myself. In some ways, that season forced me into vulnerability. We were so outside our comfort zone, moving so quickly, that there was no other way to move forward together. Yet that willingness, no matter how terrified it could make me feel, was how I found my way to deeper truths about who I am and what I'm capable of. For a while, I was surprised every time I felt my soul rise to the occasion. But do it enough times, and you find yourself opening more of those doors willingly.

LESS THAN A HANDFUL of years ago, Chip and I were a couple of seasons away from launching Magnolia Network, and the idea of my own cooking show came up in conversation. Food and time spent in the kitchen have become so deeply ingrained in the life of our family that the idea of doing our own kind of cooking show felt like a natural extension of who we are and what we value. But it meant being willing to share a sacred space with a world of strangers. And filming it without Chip right beside me meant I'd have to carry an entire show on my own. The closer we got to filming, the more anxious I became. I was questioning everything—what people would think, my ability. Doubting whether I could do it alone with dozens of people staring at me from behind a camera. Reminding everyone around me that I am not a professional chef, I didn't go to culinary school. I'm just a home cook who enjoys messing around in the kitchen and making meals for her kids.

The first day we filmed the show, old fears triggered fast. I stood at the island and immediately felt like that kindergartner standing at the front of the class holding a button in my hand. With every word I said, I found myself looking up, gauging the faces staring back at me—hoping I was saying all the right things.

While filming the entire first season, which lasted about a month, fear and I did a dance again a few times over. Insecurities from high school, the ones that started to take root in kindergarten, would shoot straight to the surface of my heart. But then, that deeper truth: I love to cook, and I love spending time in the kitchen. Sure, it was uncomfortable for me to step into a space and admit that I was probably going to do some things completely wrong, that I'm not an expert at this whole cooking thing. But that was never the heart of the show. Because it isn't for experts. It's for other people like me, who want to enjoy time in the kitchen *and* make a good meal for their families— people who might see my willingness to show a little of the mess and the fun you can have along the way and feel like they can too.

I think there is power in asking *why* when it comes to choosing one courageous yes after another. When we can align with our heart's desire, and see there's something beautiful here—something worthy of the work, even the potential discomfort. Whether it's a kind ambition or beautiful intention, your *why* can soften your fall. Wrangle yours however you need to. Maybe it's by sharing it with a friend or a spouse. Or whispering it to yourself on the side of the road until you believe it's true. The more you speak, or the more you write, the more willing you'll be to push aside fear and walk forward in truth.

When I think back to that moment I decided to start the blog, or when I said yes to my first design project, and every time I've said yes since—showing up even though I wasn't an expert, when I didn't know for sure if I could rise to the occasion—walking through each door is what led me to the next opportunity. Now I can see it as the recurring theme in my life every time I have been willing to open up and grow someplace new. And only when I started to string these chapters of my life together could I see that vulnerability is why I am here, but also what led me here—wanting to share my story with you.

MY OWN RESOLVE with vulnerability exists mostly on paper—writing and writing until fear has no place on the page. I've shared that writing has been a tool I've used every morning for the past thirty years to get out of my head and put my thoughts on paper so I can glean perspective in plain sight. Where what's left is intent. The *why*. The sincerity behind putting myself out there. Not the crap the world would have me believe, but the true ways of my heart.

I think, more than anything, what tends to reveal itself is what lies beneath those feelings of fear, whether it's fear of failure or of not being accepted or of unknowns. I can see that what I'm really struggling with are insecurities about not being good enough, or not being worthy. Maybe to you those seem like much more difficult realities to come to terms with. I've felt that same way. It can be overwhelming to acknowledge that my pursuit of perfection or my instinct to protect myself from failure really comes down to times when I haven't felt worthy of showing up simply as I am.

Yet every time I do, and I stand in truth—my heart and arms open wide—I'm reminded that I was made to feel more than just afraid. I can also be brave. And, more often than not, the two go hand in hand. I think most of us are far more capable of this—feeling more than one way at once. I think we can be tender *and* ambitious. Sensitive *and* strong. Shy *and* vocal. Fearful *and* courageous. That has been my experience with vulnerability. It lets us feel one, then shows us how to become the other.

That sort of hope is what steadies my every step during moments of doubt. When I find myself looking over my shoulder, wondering who's watching me or what people will think. Moments when fear has gripped me—knowing I am more than a moment of fear or insecurity, that this doesn't have to be where things end.

This is how we begin to trust our own instinct over criticism. Our own intuition over doubt. It's how we muster the courage to fact-check what we already feel deep down in our bones, to know if it's worth clinging to. And it doesn't always have to look like living out loud. Sometimes it looks like standing firm, holding to those convictions and ideals, because that can be brave too.

None of this is for the faint of heart. It costs us something when we choose to live open-hearted and out of our shadow side. We have to lean into discomfort, deal with our emotions head-on. Shatter perceptions of who we've been. But also uncover who we were meant to be.

Even as I think back to the season when I started to sense this book on the horizon, my immediate reaction was fear, stemming from insecurity and doubt. It took me an entire year of voice memos and writing down bits and pieces of these chapters in my journal before it felt right in my heart. Knowing it is in your hands still scares me a little.

But then, that deeper truth: I'll keep writing because of the hope I have in it.

One more thing before you close this chapter and move on to another. This way of living can feel like this great big uncovering. A stripped-down show in the middle of a crowded street. But try to remember all the times you've been gutsy in the midst of uncertainty. When you took the job you didn't think you could do. When you scaled back or changed course. When you started a family. Vulnerability was there every time you asked for forgiveness or offered compassion. It's been with you every time you've sought truth or resisted the status quo. The first time you chose to stand up for yourself. Then for someone else. And every time after that.

There will be times when we are sure enough that walking through unknown doors will feel easy. But not always. Other times, courage of that nature will feel a million miles away. I've had to learn what fear feels like so I can recognize when it's moving in. Some days I'm quick to push it aside, and other days I'm persuaded to backslide to old ways.

Chances are, you'll win some and you'll fail some too. I can't know what you're hiding from. Or what triggers cause you to shrink up and steal away in the safety of your shadow. Or whether it comes from a moment of sincere pain or has morphed into something make-believe. I only know that we all have them, and that giving fear the final word will only ever keep us running for cover.

I hope for both of us that when fear does come rushing in, we'll be wise enough to question what's behind it. And whether it's shame, uncertainty, or a sense of unworthiness, we'll remember that, as powerful as those emotions are, we are not powerless to them. They are ours to hold and to own and to wrestle to the ground. Even when they look and act and sound like protection, they are what keep us from living life with our whole hearts.

I also hope we'll remember that discomfort means we're making progress, and vulnerability, in all its messiness, is the only way to move forward. And maybe more than anything, I hope we'll both remember that this is how we tell our story—in search of truth. In plain sight. So we may live and share our lives in full.

This kind of living means admitting that we are complex, that we can feel two ways at once, that our lives are messy, and that we don't have it all figured out. But when we live like this, that magical something happens. We see that we're not alone. For some, vulnerability will come by way of grand gestures. But not for all of us. It won't always feel like a lightning-strike moment or fireworks in the sky. Sometimes, it's forged in patience, steady and unhurried. But know that when you do choose to make a move, even at a tip-toe pace, others will follow.

None of us has to go on fighting monsters in the dark by ourselves. We can show one another that it's safer to live open-hearted after all.

Out of hiding. Willing to step forward courageously even when there's no guarantee—only a hope that the life we're worthy of abounds on the other side. Whether we leap forward or put one brave foot in front of the other.

Fear breaks. We rise.

WE CAN BE

Tender *and* ambitious. Sensitive *and* strong. Shy *and* vocal. Fearful *and* courageous.

That's the gift of vulnerability. It lets us feel one, then shows how

TO BECOME THE OTHER.

CHAPTER THREE

Bridges

For a while, I was good at building fortresses, good at establishing one sturdy wall of self-protection after another. I knew how to retreat, and for most of my life, I considered it a safety measure. But once you let vulnerability seep through those walls, once you give away your heart, bring a child into the world, share your work with someone, all bets are off. When I became a mom, I had this immediate sense of how fragile those walls were, how easily they could come crashing down around me, taking with them every layer of facade and performance. Leaving in their wake all the minutes and days and years and decades of pain and shame unresolved. There is something about that intimate connection to someone who is part *you*, whose life depends on the health of your own, that can make you think twice about what you have to offer them.

The problem with walls is that they shield you from feelings of pain and shame, maybe, but also goodness, also beauty. I'd always believed I was protecting myself for good reason, but walls that tall mean only ever giving your heart in pieces. As a new mom I was starting to realize that the fortress I'd built, while safe and sturdy, didn't allow for doors to open or roads to enter in. It was a survival plan for one. But now I had a family, kids, who needed to be able to see me—*all of me*—and that had me looking for a way out.

I'VE BEEN THINKING a lot about survival. About what makes us run for cover, why we retreat or build walls. Recent history has certainly warranted thoughts about how we, as human beings, instinctually pull through difficult situations and try to move forward. I've wondered what it is that courses through our bodies in moments of upheaval. Why some fight while others flee, why we avoid putting ourselves out there—whether it's fear of failing, of not fitting in, of *fill in the blank*. And I think it goes back to pain. But also, stories.

Pain from our past seems to prey on uncertainty. When I think back to those early days as a mom, feeling fragile, feeling unsure, but also feeling a mix of excitement and exhaustion, gratitude and awe.

A lot of those feelings are back. As I've said, I'm in a season of my life when I can sense change on the horizon. I have a desire to take control again of the story I'm writing with my life, feeling uncertain about what these next handful of years should look like. I didn't know what to call it at twenty-one. I do now. I know it's vulnerability that has me feeling a little weak in the knees. At the same time, I can also sense a temptation to give in to familiar villains—fear, namely—telling me it's safer to go back to old ways of self-protecting in the midst of uncertainty. And it's in that precious gap, I'm learning, that pain from our past makes its move, in search of those crevices, that it finds the places where you're exposed, and it flows in with the strength of a river. And it's in that precious gap that we'll tell ourselves those well-worn stories, the ones that can always keep us held in suspension: *Don't let that happen again.* Don't let yourself be called a name, don't remind people that you're different. Don't show your work to anyone. But mostly, don't step into unknowns because no one will be there to catch you.

I bet you know the stories I'm talking about—the ones we tell ourselves right before we choose to risk, to be brave, to trust. Or perhaps, directly following a situation or conversation that doesn't go the way we expected. Stories about all the ways something could go wrong or all the ways it did, why that person gave you a weird look or walked away frustrated. Why they broke your heart.

Think about the last time you felt a little jaded—a little hurt or shamed. What story did you tell in that moment? Were you gentle enough with yourself to consider your blind spots, all the parts of the equation that you don't know and can't see? Or, when left to your own imagination, did that story boil down to conclusions about your value and worth, and leave you feeling more insecure than ever about who you are and whether you're enough?

I can point to a handful of times I've done this recently. Where a conversation left me guessing intent rather than asking if I'd guessed wrong, or even if I'd guessed right. Instead, that story sinks into my head and into my heart as truth, when really, without knowing the facts, it's nothing more than a theory. Nothing more than make-believe. Yet this is why we'll learn to guard ourselves, why we'll go on building castles in the sand.

But then, one day when the walls come crashing down, we're forced to look at all those stories we've told ourselves, forced to see all the ways we haven't healed. I've come to learn that when I don't find resolve, there's nowhere for the hurt to go—so it stays inside me, wreaking havoc on my sense of worthiness. Or, worse, it gets projected onto someone who doesn't deserve it. And offloading pain in the name of protection doesn't sound like a fair trade to me. In fact, it sounds like the path to continual hurt.

I know that's not the heart of most of us. I think it's more likely that we don't know what to do with open wounds. We don't really know how to heal, or we have an idea but can't move ourselves to take the time and go through the discomfort of making it right. So we push it down, carry on, and quietly blame our pain every time we choose comfort over living courageously.

In writing this book, though, and in going back over some of my own hurt these past two decades, I have come to a different theory about the purpose of pain. I'm not so sure anymore that it haunts us with only bad intentions. I'm beginning to see that its echo resounds to make sure we're listening to what it has to teach us. That in the reliving, we can connect the dots of ways we've been hurt. Seek similarities, dig into nuances, discover how one painful moment became a bridge to a better understanding of who we are and what we should be fighting for.

Maybe, like me, you've learned to see that pain that originated in your childhood isn't all that different from the pain you felt last week. Maybe the circumstances were different, but the pain was the same. It's like how we all bear a certain purpose and certain gifts, and often only in hindsight can we see the invisible string running through our lives that has led us to where we are. I think the same holds true for our pain. I've started to wonder if there are certain soft spots in all our souls. It could be loneliness, or a sensitivity to body image. An obsession with success that, if you really dug down, goes back to someone from middle school who told you you'd never become something. Certain hang-ups that run deep. We're not all just walking around afraid of everything. The reasons we're so easily triggered days, years, decades later no longer seem like coincidence or even like retribution. I think it may be gentler than that, more purposeful—the world's way of reminding us that the pain we carry, though it comes from our past, doesn't mean it isn't someone else's present. That rarely is pain a one-off experience, but rather something we share. The pain you may feel right now? Chances are there's someone else out there who bears those same scars.

There are, within each of our histories, inevitable cracks that need filling, fractures that need mending. How we begin to make repairs in the aftermath is up to us. We can fill the crevices with the things that may seem easiest at first glance—the rubble, the ash, the stuff of life that ends up doing us more harm than good. Or we can dig deeper, past the surface, till we find the specks of gold hidden in the dust.

Perhaps some of your pain is feeling within reach. Maybe you've already begun writing some of it down in a journal. Maybe you've written it right onto the pages of this book. Anywhere works. Physically find those pages. Look at that pain. This time, we're going to inch even closer to it. I can't promise it won't hurt more at first, but learning how to wield my pain for good is the only way I've known to find lasting healing. So I want you to dance with your grief. I want you to let your heart sink into it. Let that ugliness—whatever it is—cycle in, and then again and again until it cycles out. Until you start to feel something different, something new.

Get curious about those new emotions that rise. Can you see anywhere history repeats itself? Certain triggers that have hurt you again and again? Connect those dots—find out what's been festering at the bottom of your heart for who knows how long. Do you know a little something about the sting of loneliness? Have you been called a name that didn't seem fair—more than a few times? Have your own beautiful intentions been misinterpreted or misconstrued? You likely have enough examples to fill a chapter of your own. I've now walked through this process of writing down my story twice in my life, and interestingly enough, both times the same themes have risen to the surface: insecurity about my identity and fear of not being good enough. But this is the transformative part: consider how you could give your pain purpose, how you might wield it for good. What difficulty from your own life do you see mirrored in the life of someone around you? Let that pain matter after all the years you've held it. Let it be worthy of the weight you've carried by turning it into empathy for those still walking its path.

AS I THINK BACK now to my younger self, my heart breaks for what I know she'll go through. But there is also the promise of what I know she'll learn—that thirty years later she won't wish away the pain she lived through because she knows something of the gift it bears.

Once I knew how to name my pain, I could more easily recognize it in others. I learned how it felt to carry empathy—true, genuine, I've-been-in-your-shoes empathy. Not sympathy, and not pity. Empathy is where I've found purpose, and being able to bridge my experience to someone else is where I've found healing. Empathy has been my path forward. It's right there in the word, after all.

To carry empathy is to know pain and hurt. And to wield it requires rising above that pain and hurt. Neither are easy. But a fortress will only ever keep us safe for a time, and is only ever good for hiding, not healing.

Bridges, however, by their very nature, carry us forward. They connect us, first to our own story, then to the stories of others. Knowing something of the alternative, the loneliness and isolation that comes with self-protection, I can say that I'm willing to build bridges of empathy till my hands give out. Because now I believe that bridge by bridge is how we survive.

I DIDN'T GROW UP with a great understanding of what empathy means. I think I often confused it with sympathy and have now learned it can also masquerade as pity pretty easily. I've had to learn that it's neither sympathy nor pity. Nor is it a promise to problem solve—and I'm a fixer by nature. In certain relationships in my life, I've met someone's problems with ways of solving them. And when I couldn't, or it seemed like they weren't healing quickly enough, I became apathetic. But I'm learning that empathy isn't about fixing people. It's not even something to *do*. Not some grand gesture for all to see. Empathy is recognizing the burden someone is bearing, extending grace and understanding, and being present in it with them, knowing something of the load they're carrying.

Just a few weeks ago, Chip and I were having dinner with a couple of old friends—people we've come to respect and really admire. About halfway through dinner, we got to a few more serious topics, and it led Chip and me to share a few things we'd been grieving for the past couple of years. Different issues, but ones we'd both felt weighed down by. We talked and talked for a while, baring our souls in a way from across the table. We slowed down a bit, both getting out what we felt we needed to, and we looked over at our friends, wondering what words of wisdom they'd bestow on us, curious how they might encourage us to move past each of these particular hurts. But they said nothing for what felt like forever. The silence lasted so long I almost changed the subject to what we were having for dessert. But something kept me quiet. Chip too. And as the silence grew so long, I started to understand its purpose. They weren't quick to fix our grief because they'd known something of it themselves. They let us sit with it, let it do what it needed to. Not resistant—I think they knew that only ends up hurting more. The silence sort of ended up validating our sadness. I can't speak for Chip, but I began to heal at that moment. The pain no longer felt uncontrollable or insurmountable. I was able to put a name to it.

As much silence as there was that night, our friends' point rang loud. Healing often looks like quiet. Like sitting and feeling and really processing what you need to. I think so many people are quick to skirt that part, but then wonder why that pain keeps them up at night, and why that grief keeps them from living life to the fullest. But this is how we heal—by feeling our way through it. And empathy is much the same—showing others you're willing to sit in it too, that there's no shame in pursuing honest understanding. For ourselves and among one another. Shoulder to shoulder, or across the table.

Perhaps empathy has been extended to you without your recognizing it. I think you know by the way it feels when someone seeks forgiveness or freely offers it to you. By the way it feels when someone looks you in the eye with interest, instead of opposition. I've known it by the way my own heart is softened in moments when someone has truly listened. Because empathy isn't loud or flashy. It's often exchanged in quiet. And it doesn't discriminate. If you have known pain or hurt in your life, or if you've ever felt misunderstood, you carry its power. I have a feeling that's most of us.

Yet somewhere along the road to adulthood, it felt safer to leave behind a willingness to allow sadness to wash over us, to sit in grief, to invite disappointment to linger while we contemplate where it's really coming from. In its place, many of us picked up a resistance to anything that might make us feel less than happy. It's not that I don't believe in happiness, but when it becomes the sole pursuit of life, I can't help but wonder what we might be missing out on in the process: the potential to learn more—through our failures, through our sadness and grief—about who we are, what runs deep, and how we can best help this hurting world.

I've come to believe that our pain has a lot to say about our purpose. My history doesn't put me in a place to carry empathy in every lane of pain or every matter of the heart. In areas where my own history doesn't intersect with another's, I don't pretend to understand what they're going through. In those moments, I do hope to have sympathy and compassion, to learn and to gain understanding. But when I recognize a pain that I know deep in my bones, or a similar hurt whose scars I still bear, that's where I believe I should be serving.

If I hadn't experienced those lonely days as the new kid at my high school, I wouldn't be able to recognize the sting of loneliness. The kids who feel like no one's noticing them, who are sitting alone in their own world, wanting to scream that they're just trying to survive. I have a heart for that, having known how that felt even as a grade-school kid who was made to feel less than for looking different. So now when my kids go to school, I can tell them who to look for, how to reach out, what that kid might be needing. Because I was one of them. Again, the circumstances might be different, but the pain is the same.

My girls are about the age where my own insecurities really started to take root. The same ones I'm still learning how to break. Sometimes they say things, even fleetingly, about something someone said, and it's like I'm back in middle school, right there with them. But instead of shushing the insult that hurt them, or trying to overcompensate with a compliment, I'm learning to say, "I used to believe that lie too. I get it. I know how it feels and I'm here to work through it with you if you want me to." Hopefully, they'll let me walk them back to a place of trusting their own voice over someone else's.

Insecurities around my identity have also transformed my heart and my perspective for those who feel less-than. I empathize with people who know what it's like to overhear quiet insults directed at them, who pretend not to notice the sideways glances, the wandering eyes. People who feel like they have to break themselves down to fit into the box the world tells them to, the same box I'd squeezed myself into more times than I care to remember. I know I'm not the only one who has felt this way—misunderstood, misrepresented, or missed all together. So the last thing I would ever want anyone to believe is that I'd throw rocks at you for being different.

These past few years, though, I've learned yet another lesson about what I cannot control, about how easily my words can get twisted, how often my intentions can be misconstrued. Being in the spotlight has that effect. It's become a reality of ours to see stories about us, about things we've said or done, that couldn't be further from the truth. Sometimes it's like I can feel this barrier between me and the truth, and I hate that I can't do much about it. Especially when it ends up hurting someone whose pain I empathize with the most. People I would never want to think I'm not for them.

There's always a part of me that wants to scream the truth from the mountaintops, that wants to fix the narrative because I *thought* we all were grown-ups who learned how to play fair. But empathy is teaching me another way forward. It's reminding me that screaming from the mountaintops would just be more noise. And that trying to right wrongs these days only seems to add fuel to the fire. I'm learning that true and lasting healing comes when I'm determined to extend empathy. Not anger, not bitterness or resentment over what I cannot fix. Those emotions won't withstand the long haul of the journey I'm on.

I've come to see that a huge piece of my place in this world is to highlight passionate people who are doing beautiful things. To shine a light on the diverse tapestry God has woven together. The way I see my work—from the stories we tell in the magazine and on the network—is to showcase talents and passions from all corners of our world. Different religions, unique ways of living, perspectives that will make us all think differently. I've come to believe that an interesting world is far better than one that looks and thinks just like you or me. Every quirk and difference that sets us apart from one another matters to the gifts we carry because they're part of our story. It's what we bring to the world—and it's what makes it a more beautiful place.

This feels especially important at this moment. As a culture, it feels like we're struggling to see people as people—with beating hearts, flesh and bones, layered in wonder. But simply as right or wrong. Forgetting that we are real and complex human beings whose stories run deep. That we are more than this or that. And that reason and meaning and truth often sit below the surface.

But once you try, once you really empathize with someone's experience and where they're coming from, that's when compassion rises up; that's when resolution and resolve rise up. If we spend our time going back and forth just so you hear me and I hear you, rarely are we ever going to come to a place of peace.

But choose empathy, choose understanding, and it destroys the assumption that *different* means we have nothing in common. In its place, it rebuilds what has always been far truer: there is more that bonds us than breaks us.

I've had to learn for myself that where I have pain, I also have power and a place to empathize. It's something you'll have to learn for yourself too. It can be a vulnerable thing to recognize where we carry empathy, and then to will ourselves to give it away.

I'VE HAD TO LEARN an important sequence: in order to empathize with someone else I have to first offer myself that same grace. In big ways, this has looked like finding healing for the things that have hurt me, but it's a daily practice in smaller ways too. I'm a perfectionist, so my bent is toward seeing only what I missed, looking back on each day at all the should-haves and could-haves. Empathy for myself in those moments looks like practicing gratitude for what I did do, simply because it was the best of me—the best of what I had to offer. I have found myself unable to extend empathy the way I intend, with grace and patience, when I'm unwilling to grant that same favor to myself, when I don't give my own heart that same time to get right. To let my own thoughts cycle in, bringing with them whatever I'm feeling at the surface, until they settle deeper and deeper—deep enough for me to understand where they're really coming from.

I'll be the first to admit the path to healing can be tiring. I'm the checklist type. I like to cross things off and keep on moving. But there's nothing quick about healing. About learning to speak kindly to yourself. At first, it can feel like there's nothing quick about honest understanding of another's point of view, either.

I think about my youngest son, Crew. When he falls or trips or gets a cut, I can be quick to want to fix his pain, quick to place a Band-Aid over it and tell him it's all better now. But he will say to me, "No, Mommy, it still hurts." A simple reminder that he needs the Band-Aid, but also a kiss, as well as a breath or two to heal. Not the wound, necessarily, but the way it made him feel.

Chip and I practice this between the two of us. When we're in a discussion or an argument, I have to remind myself to slow down my racing mind. To let go of my pride. To let go of my need to be right. Or to fix things. But to listen readily, to really hear him out. Chip is a fixer by nature too. If there's something hurting me, his instinct can be to problem solve on my behalf. But we're both learning the value of quiet, of unhurried resolve, of patiently asking questions instead of offering answers, of sitting in silence, just to feel another's pain together.

I've seen this play out from the other side too, most recently with our oldest kids, who now as teenagers need us to help them heal no longer with a Band-Aid and a kiss but by simply being there. Learning how we're supposed to show up for our children, season to season, can feel like a never-ending game of trial and error. Whatever playbook you have for them—at five, eight, twelve—is outdated before you ever fully learned the rules. Not to mention that each kid is so incredibly distinct. I've never known a parenting tip that's one-size-fits-all. And when it comes to pain our kids feel, I gather I'm not the only one who jumps to help heal, to want to fix whatever is aching their young hearts. When they were small, I know I was often quick to dismiss any discomfort they might be feeling. And it's sad to me to admit this, but I've watched how some of our kids slowly stopped coming to me with their problems and their pain, tired of me always trying to fix them. To heal whatever wound they had. On some days, that reality has felt like an assault on motherhood. Isn't it our job to protect, to nurture? I believe those traits were poured into my being the day I became a mom. But with each one of our kids, I'm learning that the older they get, it's less about what I can offer them and more about how I sit with them. How we listen and wait is sometimes as essential as how we shape. Showing up for my oldest few right now doesn't look like solving their problems or fixing their pain. Instead, I've learned that when I can be the person on the other side of whatever hurt they're bearing, willing to listen and wait, to sit in it with them, it's a profound thing I get to witness. I get to watch them cycle through their pain long enough for it to then cycle out. I get to watch them discover on their own the root of their hurt. I get to see them be the hero of their own story.

We all deserve that. And I've started to believe that it's how Chip and I send these five beautiful kids out into the world well, where they're willing to bear their own cracks because they know how to make repairs—and where they're willing to sit in the pain of another's because they know the process themselves.

THERE IS PLENTY to keep us from ever going there. Partly because it takes some digging. This kind of pain usually sits deep, and the real heartache takes some discovery. If it's a muscle that's rarely used, it will take practice. Then there's the matter of being willing to sit in someone else's mess without trying to fix it that can cause discomfort too, some getting used to. Our culture makes this easy to avoid. Humanity in general isn't great at being curious about emotion. We *are* fixers and cover-uppers. We pull ourselves up by our bootstraps, or at least we're told those who do go the furthest.

But to me, the riskier alternative is not finding the space to heal, and not granting that same favor to others—because we can see how hiding out, covering up our pain, and building walls of self-protection is threatening our spirits, our hopes, our joy, our ability to live shoulder to shoulder. When we don't learn what we need to push aside—whether it's fear, feelings of unworthiness or uncertainty, pain of any kind—when we don't meet those lies with vulnerability or do the hard work of rewriting them with truth, we end up perpetuating our pain or projecting it, hurting not just ourselves but more people in the crossfire.

I believe that at our core, we are all more similar than we think. That we all long to be seen. Plainly. And loved just as we are. We long to be known more intimately than we sometimes let ourselves show. And those desires can be quickly short-circuited by past pain, past hurt, the idea that no one has ever shown us empathy before, so why should we.

Sometimes the first bridge to understanding will have to be one of your own making. Surer, steadier, with every vulnerable and willing step. But do that, let it carry you across, and I promise you there will be more bridges ahead. More hands there next time to help clear the path forward.

For me, the straightest way back to empathy will always be story, constantly reminding myself there is more to know of those around me. I believe there are opportunities to extend empathy every day, and I know I'm guilty of missing many of them. It's not such an easy task in the world we live in. Our social culture is robbing us of deep and true connection—of joy, peace, and honest understanding of both ourselves and one another. But every day I have a choice: I can either perpetuate the pain I carry, or I can give it purpose by living with an empathetic posture. It's something I have to fight for daily, with a willingness to dig a little deeper into my own heart to find all the places where pain lives, and to listen a little more to the pain points of others. Empathy isn't something I've mastered, but as I reach for it more and more— over regret, over bitterness, over indifference—I've found it to be there waiting whenever I'm willing.

I wish I would have known the gift that pain bears earlier in my life. I would have wasted fewer years letting past hurt shroud who I am and what purpose I have to offer this world.

But now, today, and moving forward, I no longer have to fear pain because I know its power. I've walked across my own bridge, and it's led me to a better understanding of myself and my story. And it's there that I got to see how much more belonging and love and being seen exists when we're willing to build the next bridge together. Pain may be the most common thread between us at first, but I believe it is through this same lens that we begin to see what else we share—dreams, intentions, hopes, triumphs. More reasons to live *for* one another.

As I step forward into the next season of my life, this is what I know to be true: Empathy is the only way we move forward intact. It's the only way we restore understanding and reclaim shared moments of goodness, of humor, of lightness—of a culture that feels like it's on our side. I can't imagine a world where it doesn't move the needle. I can't imagine us coming out on the other side of every bridge and not being made stronger because of it, not taking better care of ourselves and one another because of it, not finding healing because of it. And I can't imagine that not being the greatest story we ever write together.

A fortress will only ever keep us safe for a time,

and is only
ever good
for hiding,
not healing.

CHAPTER FOUR

Look
Up

A few days passed as a stack of mostly blank pages sat idly on my desk. I'd been trying to write down everything I could remember from the first handful of years of life as a family. It would have been the late 2000s, and Chip and I had brought home four babies in five years. A few scenes came to mind pretty easily, mostly pieced together from what I'd seen captured in photos—the fairy garden–themed birthday party we threw for Ella's birthday, and Christmas at my parents' house. The soft yellow color of our first home, all eight hundred square feet of it. But the moments between some of those milestones—that's where things got hazy. Anything else I'd start to remember felt so far away, I could only see it in shapes, blurred once by too much time and again by too much distance. It was like I couldn't get close enough to separate them from one another, to know what I should write down. So I ended up jumping ahead in years, and as I was weaving in and out of family trips, first days of school, and the way our business grew alongside us, I had to pause when I got to 2018.

That was a year like no other. Chip and I had been running for a while—maybe fifteen years. Those four babies had become kids and teenagers, we'd grown a business, found ourselves on a television show, and were constantly in the middle of a project. We loved all of it, for the most part, but it was starting to show that we wouldn't be able to keep pace much longer. *Fixer Upper* had just aired its fifth and what we thought would be its final season, and our business was asking for every inch of us. And so, in the summer of 2018, Chip and I looked at each other, feeling out of breath, and agreed our family needed a rest. Our bodies and our souls were *tired.* We told our team and our friends that we were going to take some time off.

Only two weeks later, I found out I was pregnant. As much as Chip and I had joked about the possibility of having another child, I truly believed I was done. And yet, eight years after my last pregnancy, there I was—forty years old with a newborn in my arms.

Middle-of-the-night feedings weren't exactly what I'd had in mind for our season of rest, and those foggy first months of newborn life had me feeling like a first-time mom all over again. Only this time, things felt different. With Crew's little body pushed up against mine, something inside me was saying, *Stay close.* I could stare for hours and hours at his tiny fingers and toes. Comforted by the way his small breaths could steady my own. As I came out of a series of seasons that always had me running, Crew was slowing me down.

As hard and good and exhausting as those early days were, looking back, it's sweet how we were given exactly what we needed for that exact moment in time, even in the most unpredictable ways. Crew *was* rest. For the first time in a long time, I was living only for the moment in front of me. His tiny presence was prompting me to look up, to catch every little wonder. He had my heart, and I would come to realize just how much he would change it from the inside out.

WHEN I THINK BACK to the beginning, our first four kids were born in such quick succession that, honestly, it's no surprise it was all a bit of a blur. Chip and I had only been married a couple of years when we had our first son, Drake, and within four years, our family had grown by three more. Time and money and sleep were all scarce, and I remember greeting each of those babies with a mix of excitement, uncertainty, exhaustion, and awe.

From there, life only seemed to pick up. As much as I want to believe that somewhere in the dusty recesses of my mind there are clear and distinct memories—the way my heart swelled the moment they took their first wobbly steps, the feel of their little hand tucked into mine, notes of precious things they've said—every year those seem to fade a little more. Of course, I've held on to school art and keepsakes and photos throughout the years, but I can't so easily recall those tender little moments, the ones I think you find yourself wishing you could will to memory later, after years have passed. Just to breathe them in again. To feel that part of your life once more.

As I stared at those blank pages on my desk, I knew how so very true that was.

I wouldn't change a thing about the way we grew our family, but as those years ticked by, the chaos was only amplified with every dream we chased, all while trying to figure out how we wanted to grow up ourselves. When we were in our early thirties, there already was so much going on in our lives. I was learning how to be a mom and a designer at the same time. We had multiple businesses we were trying to get off the ground with very little money to our names. We were raising babies and chasing dreams, and I can't help but look back at that season of our lives and think to myself, *We were just trying to survive.*

I've mentioned that I coped with so much being out of my control by seeking it elsewhere—the way our home looked, the parties we hosted, even our daily schedules. And I built structure around our lives to try to keep us "safe" from all the stuff the world throws at us. I controlled and I micromanaged whatever I could get my fingers on—toys my kids left behind, every streak and stain left on our kitchen countertops, our to-do lists and daily activities. I think I ended up creating so much structure around our lives that I wasn't able to see it close-up, beyond the walls I'd built with my own two hands.

All the while, time moved on. And I kept living for all that people could see—the way things looked, the structure we lived in, the next you-name-it. Over the years, I've had to remind myself to cut that young mom some slack. Even now, I can see why it might have felt impossible *not* to live for what was next—not when what was next meant either feast or famine for our family. So I kept my eyes fixed forward, at the next flip, the next paycheck, believing things would slow down once we were a little more comfortable financially, or once that project was finally finished. There was always something on the horizon, and I told myself that as soon as we were over the peak, the valley would offer peace.

The problem was, I was searching for slow and reaching for rest, but still running in circles, still lying awake at night, my mind humming to the highlight reel of to-dos. I had yet to learn that life, in all its needs and nuances, is extraordinarily complex. Change, even more so.

When Crew came along, the weight of things started to shift. I was older, more confident and comfortable in my own skin, and realizing that some of the qualities that I'd relied on for most of my life that made me productive and successful were no longer serving what I wanted my future to look like. Sure, maybe some of those beliefs about who I needed to be—efficient, put together, polished—had helped us through the hectic years of building a family and a business, but now they were keeping me from what I wanted to *feel* again:

peace, presence, and an intimate connection to the very things that matter most to me.

Crew felt like a sudden gust of wind that could send me in a new direction. I didn't know where right away, but I had a feeling there would be things I'd bump up against this time around, and I'd do them differently. Most of them I couldn't have put words to then, but I knew I wanted to see things this time that had been in my blind spot before. What I longed for was a sense of presence—a way of actually feeling the moments that unraveled around me—but back then I don't think I could have put a name to it. I didn't fully understand what I was missing, but I knew Crew was teaching me how it felt to dwell deeply, to breathe in a moment until I felt it sink into me. And I knew that whatever that feeling was, I wanted more of it.

In the four years since, Crew has found his way deep into my soul, where a few of those walls still stand tall. He's grabbed my hand and invited me to follow him up and over each one.

It's amazing to me how his whole life perspective is so entirely without pretense—he admires not just the flowers when we take a walk through the garden, but the dirt and soil they grow from. When my mind is quick to want to move on, Crew pulls me back in, helping me see how even the tiniest things can be worthy of our time. His natural curiosity can draw out my own, and his reasons for getting onto his hands and knees to "see" is always reason enough for me too. Whenever I sense that old tendency to overextend just an inch more, Crew is there to remind me of the small joys that can only be noticed in pause.

Piece by piece, I am breaking down those walls I worked so hard to create around myself and our family. It took some time for me to realize that the way of living I'd tied us to might have kept us on track. I'm sure there were seasons when we needed it. But control steals joy. And structure *all the time* ends up shielding you from the fullness of life. In its place, I'm holding out for moments to simply be delighted, to let a moment of beauty catch me by surprise, to pause on something and let my thoughts linger there a while. By no means have I perfected this new way of living. But since Crew came home four years ago, I've learned enough of this beautiful new reality that I know it's what I want more of.

I've come to find that a journey like this one is messy and winding. It's trickier than I anticipated, to choose only what's in front of me in a world that spins on distractions. It has meant unlearning decades of living for the high of hurry. And old habits die hard, so I'm still very much a work in progress. I've been distracted and I've missed moments. I've let perfectionism win scenarios and busyness steal seconds of true joy. I've kept my head down when I should have looked up. But these days, I recognize when I'm doing it, I can sense when I've missed it, and I simply begin again.

Maybe not every moment will be worthy of the attention—but for the most part, the ones I've caught these past few years I wouldn't have wanted to miss. And it's made me more aware of how many small joys are happening all around us on a daily basis, and how many of them we fail to experience when we're busy looking down.

THIS IS NOT TO SAY there isn't plenty that keeps our eyes fixed on our feet. We live in a world that isn't shy about telling us how to manage our time. We are reminded often to prioritize our kids, our marriage, our work, our friendships—but also ourselves!—which is to say that we should prioritize *everything*. And over the years, I've listened and I've tried, and I bet you have too. Because of course we all want to do right by the things we love.

But those different areas of our lives aren't small things; they are its total sum, and it can get overwhelming and tiring fast if we try to divide our days in a way that supports it all. So we make lists. We prioritize. We shift things around when time inevitably runs out. And if you're like me, when you don't get to everything, you end up feeling like you must have failed somewhere along the way.

I've started to wonder if that's where distractions take root. Right there, in the void of perceived failure and insecurity about how good of a job we're doing at this whole business of being human. It's as if our minds are more easily rerouted when things around us feel like they're falling apart. I've learned that when we're not feeding our souls with grace and truth, they feed themselves with all sorts of ugly interruptions.

We all have different tendencies toward distractions that keep us looking down. It might be an obsession with work, which is easily fed by burying ourselves deeper in it. Or maybe it's a natural inclination toward discontentment, easily fed by scrolling through social media. For me, I know I wasn't made to sit still. I genuinely enjoy having a lot on my plate. Too much downtime and I get antsy. Not enough projects and I get bored. So I fell hard for the frantic pace of a world that wears busyness like a badge of honor. And I grew up assuming my well would always run deep—deep enough to cover a life on autopilot, where I could go and go until every box was checked off, every email answered, every task complete. It didn't, of course. That's why I'm here, desperately trying to reorient my life from within.

I'll be honest, though: I spent years trying to outsmart the clock. Thinking efficiency was how you could add more hours to the day. Thinking that if I could just move faster and get everything done quicker, I'd have time to enjoy my life. Maybe you resonate with that. I doubt I'm the only one, when efficiency seems to be built into our culture's DNA. Maybe we're not officially taught it in school, but I think from a young age we begin to learn efficiency's value in this world. We're encouraged to manage our time well and then offered reminders by those older and wiser that time flies by. See the problem there? We're told to try and control what we should already know we have no hold on. For me, those lessons about efficiency cultivated a fear of misplacing what little time I thought I had. So I obsessed over the future but also longed for the past—at what will be or what has been. Always hustling toward what's next before I ever had a chance to enjoy what's present. And then, all too quickly, it became what's past. Just like those older and wiser had predicted, no matter how quickly I hustled, I would end up blaming time for moving too fast. It's easy to, when you live in fear of it. Constantly putting yourself in positions where you're wondering where it went.

It's no wonder we tend to treat time as yet another burden to carry. Pleading for more of it. Calling it a thief. Asking it to be kind. Blaming it for giving us a life that we only get to experience in hindsight.

While I let ideas around efficiency consume the first half of my life, completely un-fought, when Crew came along, I wanted to *feel* again. I was frustrated with myself for having lived in a way that blurred too much of my past. So I spent a season trying to wrestle busy out of me, feeling repulsed by my own tendency to go, go, go. But these past few years have taught me a lot about how to reconcile parts of who I am with the kind of person I want to be, having realized there's a good chance I'll always view certain aspects of my life through a lens of efficiency. It's part of how I'm wired, and there's no use fighting that. So these days I'm careful not to give my whole self over to it, and I'm learning to identify when spending my time efficiently might overshadow opportunities to spend it well. I'm in a place now where I'm learning to live among that part of me, knowing that when I can wield it in healthy ways, efficiency can make me a better wife, a better mom, a better business owner.

I think the same is true for whatever distractions have a hold on you, whatever you find yourself drawn to in moments of stress or anxiety or just plain chaos—whether it's control or perfection or something else entirely. I think there are certain instincts and skills that live in our bones, in bits and pieces that tell us something of who we are and what we're meant to offer the world. As you've probably already experienced, those impulses can be wielded for good—the pursuit of perfection can make beautiful things, control can protect us from harm or hurt, and efficiency can save us from wasted time. But too much of anything that pulls us away from life as it's happening will only ever keep us looking down.

If we don't choose for ourselves where we show up and lean in and get close, other people will. And if we don't choose to be present for the moments we truly care about, our lives could spin on distractions and interruptions till the day we die.

THE WORLD ALREADY has a lot to say about presence. Social media companies have risen on platforms that promise a convenience of connection. Giving us a way to share our everyday moments with anyone who's interested. Teaching us how we can show up in other people's lives, day or night, even a world away, with only a snap of our cameras and click of a button. Lulling us into believing that it's a simple thing to be present with such convenience.

By now we know too well how much unhealth and discontent can come from a life that's lived on a screen. A life where moments are captured only to be celebrated in a four-by-four square. Maybe ten years ago posting a photo was genuinely an act of enjoying the in-the-moments of life, but I know that for me, over the years, it's become more of a calculated decision. I've found myself critiquing messy backgrounds and blurry smiles. Snapping one photo after another until the lighting is just right, or spending too much time rewriting a caption, one that's equal parts witty and sentimental.

But a highlight reel is only ever that—the best of. It is not an honest mirror or window, because that view is always obscured to the point of only catching a glimpse. It's a snapshot in time, highly edited and beautifully presented.

There's also a certain allure to a place where we can present ourselves any way we choose with very little accountability. Where no one can tell what's real from what's artificial. And proving to strangers that our lives are built by powerful and meaningful moments tends to eclipse the real ones that are happening all around us.

I can't help but wonder what becomes of the other 95 percent of our days that are truly regular moments. The ones that may not sparkle or pop or be worthy of sharing—and yet are far more worthy than that—moments worth simply experiencing.

But *how* can we be present? Even more recently, ideas around how to be present have multiplied into new words and ways of living. *Slowness, solitude, mindfulness*—all these words, and more, tell us different ways we can embrace the here and now. And, as it is with a lot of things our culture gets its hands on—twisting and turning and spitting back out—we come up short in our own understanding.

There are magazines and podcasts dedicated to mindfulness. From all sides, we're encouraged to pursue in order to slow down. To take up yoga to become more mindful. Turn off our phones to enjoy the quiet. Walk around the block to clear our heads. Read a book to escape. Stay home to be still. Or better yet, go out to be present. Aimless directives like these can make it impossible to know what presence should look like for you and how it will be different for me. So nobody really knows how to move forward—least of all those of us who need to feel something real the most. The ones who find our value and worth in what we can get done in a day. Those whose identity hinges on how well we perform.

I don't want it to come across as though every moment is high stakes. This isn't about adding more pressure to your days by trying to make every second meaningful. But it can feel conflicting, knowing when to pause and when to go. Knowing which moments are worthy of our full attention and which ones will come around again.

Maybe it starts by getting to know who you are and the things you value stripped of the world's expectations. Determining what truly fills you up and fuels you forward. I will say, there have been seasons in my life when choosing to pause felt irresponsible. We didn't have the means to savor life, not when it felt like we were barely making it. But now, looking back, I'm convinced that it was more my idea of what presence was than our circumstance that kept me at a distance.

I viewed presence—or slowness, or solitude, whatever name you give it—as a luxury. Maybe that's the same view you hold today. Maybe it feels as elusive and far away as the day your kids will move out of the house, or as the year you finally retire. If that's where you're at, I get it. I've measured my time and my days that same way. As something to get through in hopes that there's peace and rest waiting on the other side of all we have to do. But I'm learning that presence doesn't have to steal from responsibility, not when you know what to look for.

I want to practice presence, but not just for the sake of it, and not in some aimless way. No one can afford to sit around, waiting all day on the off chance that a moment worth our time will approach us. That won't work; and besides, it feels like we'd be stripping those moments of their magic. Rather, I'm starting to see that presence doesn't have anything to do with waiting at all.

I think it's more about choosing to lean in when you could easily lean out. Letting something catch your attention instead of brushing it off—the way the light is pouring in, the carefree way your kids dance to loud music. It's recognizing a moment so beautiful that it steals your heart—and then choosing it. Over everything else. Seeing it through. Capturing the delight and wonder of the life you're tending. Go ahead and step into the sun that's shining through. Spend a moment or two in the light. Or get up and join the dance party. Let your kids see you were born for this. I think it's there you remember the other 95 percent counts for something too. Even more, that it's well worth living for.

If spontaneous moments aren't your thing, get curious about what is. A project you're passionate about. A hobby you've kept on the sidelines. Something entirely mundane. If there's something that stirs you, let it matter. Bring it to the surface so you can't so easily look away.

For me, cooking and time in the kitchen is something I crave deeply. But I've learned that if I don't first do the work of looking up, of making sure I'm connected to the moment, my head will keep on spinning with distractions and lists and all that awaits beyond the kitchen island and our table. That's why, most evenings, dinner prep looks like opening a window, lighting a candle, and turning on my favorite play-list before I've even pulled out the pots and pans. I choose to prep for presence itself. Knowing those moments matter to me, I do everything I can to make sure I don't miss them.

Maybe that sounds like a lot of work. I think sometimes it's meant to be. You don't find that rich, restorative breath if you're not willing to fight for it. For its strength lies in its depth, and sometimes I wonder if that's by design—forcing us to look beneath all of life's dizzying dis-tractions to the parts of our souls that sit a little deeper.

Think back to the last moment that made you feel something. Was it in response to something you care for? Did it break down one of those walls you've built around your life? Chances are, it was, or it did. Because moments when we feel something remind us that we're not just skin and bones. That we're not meant to be robots. Not meant to go, go, go.

As I was writing this chapter, something prompted me to step away from the desk and take a walk outside. I'm spending the day in the country. Sometimes, if I can, I like to get away to write. It's my favorite kind of Texas weather: sunny with a light drizzle. On my walk, I found a flower, completely alone. I plucked it from the ground, held it in my hand, and looked up, letting each drop of water fall on me. Cars were driving by, but I didn't care. I didn't let the thought of what people might think ruin the moment. It's sprinkling in the dead of summer and there was one flower hiding in the grass for me.

I kept the flower on my desk all weekend, as a reminder of how the simplest things can be life-giving. This practice followed me home. In moments when I feel like I'm too in my head or distracted by things I don't want to be distracted by, I'll stop and sit, and I'll look around the room I'm in. I'll say thank you for everything that is special to me: a chair made by a friend, a photo from a family trip a few years ago. My kids, if they're nearby. It's those moments of pausing to be thankful that really center me. Looking up grounds me in gratitude, and I'm just now learning that it's a really beautiful way to live.

I bet that you, too, know something of the push and pull of each day, something of the grind. Over the next couple of days, pay attention to moments that do something to your heart. Moments that make you feel again. That connect you back to a life you recognize. Whatever it may be that slows you down, stills your breath, and steadies your heart is yours and yours alone. That's where you'll feel presence waiting, only asking that you live out your precious moments just as they are—untampered with, untouched, unfolding in real time.

If yoga helps you get there, great. If reading fiction makes you feel more connected to a part of yourself, close this book for now and open that one. Do what you need to. It will be different for all of us—but the world will never know the way of our hearts like we do. And we shouldn't let it pretend that it does.

For me, this is a lesson I'm still learning. But those two simple words I'd find myself repeating in the early days of Crew's life, I still keep close whenever I feel that invariable tug to disengage from the present, to give in to some cheap distraction, to miss a moment I want to see more than anything:

Look up.

AS YOU WRITE DOWN your own story, pay attention to the moments you've kept close. Not just the scenes pulled from photographs or the highlight reel of family milestones. Those are beautiful and worthy in their own way, but when it comes to having a heart connection to the life you're living, one that you can really feel your way through, you'll have to dig a little deeper. Down to the place you've been unknowingly storing bits and pieces of beauty and wonder every time you chose to look up, to be present. Every time you were willing to abandon plans in order to catch a glimpse of something truly beautiful. When you were surprised by a moment of laughter or joy or even heartache and you thought to stay still and let it sink in for a breath or two.

My hope is that the more you write, the more you remember, the more you'll *feel* the moments themselves. That the memories you connect will inch closer and closer, one to another, and then another, until you have before you this landscape of a life you never thought you'd get to hold again.

Let that landscape reveal what you want more of. Let the story of your days so far show you what moments are worth chasing still. I know I can't go back to those early days of motherhood, but I can look out for moments that remind me that I'm a mom—and I'll let those take my breath away. Or whatever it may be for you. A friend. A partner. Proof that you're wildly creative. It's not too late to determine how you're going to live and remember the life you're building.

I've come to learn that, just like with anything that's worthwhile, presence takes practice. I'm still tempted to give in to busyness and efficiency and perfection instead of looking up.

But then, I think about Crew. About how natural it is for him to live for each moment, every curiosity only giving way to more curiosity. How easy it is for most kids because it's inherent to their nature. And how it pierces my heart to know that one day, he'll likely outgrow it. Just like I did. Just as I see our older kids beginning to. And while this pursuit of presence is something I want for myself—so I don't miss the actual fabric of our lives and the moments that, woven together, define who we are as a family—I also want it for Crew, for all of our kids.

I want it for you too.

I want us to show the world what it looks like to run opposite the hurried rhythms it has created, opposite the tide that carries us away from a life of wonder and beauty toward one of busyness and distraction. I want us to never stop trying to see more of the life we've been invited into, with the hope that the people we love never do either.

The view from where you stand is spectacular. I hope you'll look up and take it in more often than not: every breath, every sight, every sound. Because when we let our senses say to our soul, *This is something that matters to me*, we're reminded that we are more than we give ourselves credit for. That we have passions and true loves and a soul that sings, and that all those things really do mean more than the stuff that keeps us busy. It doesn't matter how late in life, how tall your walls; you have not missed your chance to see it.

LOOKING UP

grounds me in gratitude,

AND I'M JUST NOW LEARNING it's a really beautiful way to live.

CHAPTER FIVE

To Hold
and Let Go

I was combing through all the notes I have written in my journal when one caught my eye by the date that was scribbled in the corner. It was about a year and a half ago—the day Drake got his driver's license. As I started to read what I'd written down that day, I could sense the disbelief in my tone. My first baby, my son who made me a mom, was suddenly sixteen years old and about to drive away from Chip and me for the very first time.

The part that piqued my interest was toward the end. I mentioned how, earlier that day, I'd been teaching Crew, our youngest, how to step down the stairs at the house. He was about two and getting curious about our staircase, so I wanted to make sure he knew how to safely get down in case he managed to climb a step or two on his own. The dichotomy of those two realities occurring on the same day really struck me. It felt like I was letting go of my oldest in one breath, while in the next, the tiny hands of my youngest were holding on tight.

I had already been in the headspace of this chapter, thinking that if you've come this far, how could I show you that the point of writing down your story isn't all toil and sadness, slow soul work and painful journal entries. That stuff is essential; it's how we grow. But it's also just part one. It's the prologue to a life you can't wait to write about.

And as I sat there, remembering that moment, I started to make a deeper connection. Because, you see, the day we watched our oldest son drive away for the first time, I won't lie—there were a lot of tears. Not from Chip—he was practically chasing Drake down the driveway cheering him on while I went back inside to gather myself. It hurt to watch my son leave in such an obvious display of what it looks like to grow out of us. This rite of passage now belonging to him.

Yet, as I came back inside the house, I remember finding Crew, standing there as though nothing had just changed forever. He was simply wondering if I'd come back in to play with him. I don't know how to explain it other than the light softened, my heart swelled, and at that moment I knew how essential this rhythm is. To lose and then gain. To have and to hold only to let go. It was a gift of perspective. Because there was Crew, tugging on my hand to follow him, and it was this beautiful and gracious reminder of the bigger picture. Showing me that highs follow lows. That sorrow and joy can go hand in hand. That letting go reveals what else our arms were made to carry.

The same holds true for our story.

When we write it down, when we hold each piece, we get to see the full picture. The joyful seasons and heartbreaking seasons, and how one led to the other. How essential each is in making us whole. A perspective like this reminds us that life is neither completely merry nor completely tragic, but a little bit of everything all the way to its center. And that without this balancing act there'd be no tension to move us forward.

But we'll have to hold that little bit of everything for a chance at a view of the bigger picture. Without that rhythm, without that grace, we'd have no perspective, no sense of how it all works together to tell a story worthy of each of our journeys.

I'M A SELF-PROCLAIMED HOARDER. I have cupboards and drawers overflowing with collections of serveware. Linen closets stuffed full. Dozens of photo albums. Our barn sometimes doubles as storage for my favorite antiques. I don't let go of things so easily. Not when they've meant something to my family. Not even when they're no longer serving me.

When I think about all we might be holding this year, this month, this moment, it's enough to make me lose my breath. Every season brings with it beauty and goodness, and almost always some difficult and painful things too. Maybe not always in equal measure. But burdens are rarely light, and often, what we can't comfortably carry in our arms we end up pushing onto our backs, offering more space to that which is weighing us down. Inch by inch, day by day. It's impossible to put a name to all you might be holding. For me, it tends to run the gamut. Year by year, month by month, it changes as I do. But some burdens have weighed me down more than others, some heavier bricks that I willingly carried for far too long.

Pain has been my biggest learning curve. Those playground stories I'd been told—and believed—about what I should hide and who I should be manifested into insecurities about my worth. Past hurt became a weight that, for the life of me, I could not put down. It was something I might not have admitted to carrying around every day, but now I can see it for what it really was—a silent undercurrent, always there, raging just beneath the surface, veiling all the good that I was holding in a cloud of gray.

I know I spent some years trying to hold on tight to any good thing I could get my hands on, hoping that would dim the sadness, the insecurity, the uncertainty. I figured that if there was only good from where I stood, maybe my hurt would disappear. That if I could just hold the happiest pieces of my life the closest, I'd forget that deep down I didn't always feel worthy of them. Yet bringing them closer only seemed to magnify the moments from my past that convinced me I was undeserving. It took getting up close and personal with that pain, that hurt, for me to see all the good and all the beautiful scenes of my present through clear and contented eyes.

Learning how to heal, how to let go of pain and hurt and shame in healthy ways, has completely changed the way I view what I'm carrying. I spent too long reaching for safe when the world caught me by surprise, holding fear close to my chest. Figuring out how to work through my pain and put it in its rightful place—recognizing the power it carries to wield empathy—has changed my outlook, my life. It has changed the potential for what I'm capable of holding in health.

In my own life, I've also found guilt and regret to be as clingy as pain. As a mom, a spouse, a daughter, a friend, there are myriad ways I've carried guilt over my forty-four years. And like pain, guilt is hard to cut loose. It sticks to our hearts, playing navigator to our choices, our sense of goodness, our ability to judge ourselves gently. When it comes to my kids, I've been a working mom their whole lives. But they've never made me feel guilty; that's always been my own doing. When I've had to miss moments of their little lives for something going on at the office, I carry that guilt for a while. Sometimes I try to overcompensate in ways that serve no one well, gripping the wrong things even tighter as a way to reconcile my own feelings of thinking I've failed somewhere.

I wish I was the only one to carry this burden, but I gather I'm not alone. Because guilt and regret manifest in different ways every day. How could they not in the culture we live in, where efficiency is praised and status is gained by how much we can hold at once? This has made it second nature at times, for me, to focus on all the areas of my life where I think I'm failing, and at all that I'm not able to hold.

While I'm grateful for seasons of hard work and heavy loads because they show me what these arms can carry, I know I wasn't made to hold only the hard, only pain and guilt. There is more to me than that. More hope than fear. More joy than sorrow. But toil thrashes, and lack lives out loud. If we don't learn to do the hard work of letting these things go, there will never be room in our story for all the beauty it bears. I'm grateful to have found truth on the other side of lies. Vulnerability on the other side of fear. Empathy on the other side of pain. This is how I know that every season has a purpose, and that holding, even when it leads to letting go, is what clues us in to the bigger story being told.

If you believe that too—if you can hold your story in truth, for all that it is, the good and the bad, not perfect but whole—if you can see who you are as richer than any past or future thing, that's the perspective we're after. That's also the gift of writing down your story. You view where you've come from, where you stand now, and where you're going not with weariness or uncertainty but trust. Believing every piece has its purpose.

You can look ahead, ready to hold whatever ebbs and flows differently, more contentedly. Because you get, with more clarity now, what's been true all along: our story, it flows like waves. There are parts that crash down on us, moments that dance around our toes. Scenes that carry us out to sea where it's only sun and air, birds and breeze. But for every crash, every break, the tide always comes back to shore. And as I have read and reread the pages I've written on my life, decades ago, two seasons ago, this morning, I continue to be struck by the resonant truth of the message between the lines on some pages and clear as day on others: this rhythm is essential. It's where grace is. It's where peace is. But mostly, it's where our story lives.

I HAVE COME TO BELIEVE that we can learn from nature everything we ought to know about how to live in rhythm. It can be a wise teacher if we're curious enough to watch and learn how it moves—why it blooms in spring, grows wildly during summer, and yields harvests each fall, only to lay bare come winter.

Years ago, when planting a garden was only a dream in my mind, I would look out the kitchen window of our home at the empty corner of our yard and see it all in my head. I imagined a garden that was lush and abundant, overflowing with vegetables and herbs and flowers. And, like magic, that's essentially what happened during the first spring, summer, and fall that we began planting. We put in the work, and most everything went as planned. The garden was doing exactly what it was meant to do: growing, thriving, producing. It was as beautiful as I'd pictured it. Then winter settled in, and as should've been expected, everything withered. It came time to pull up all the plants and flowers that we'd grown to love, and the garden lay bare. It occurred to me that this was never a part of the dream. I never really imagined that after months of tending to it and seasons of it overflowing with life, I'd look out at the garden and just see dirt. I'll be honest: I was mad. I kind of bratted out. I wouldn't look out the window for a few weeks, feeling frustrated by this part of the process. All that beauty turned to dust. But that's what happened. And, it turns out, it's what had to happen for a chance to see it bloom again. I grew to learn how essential this rhythm of rising and falling is for the garden—but also, for all of life.

For a chance at wholeness, a chance at pursuing the full picture of who I was made to be and to live in the abundance of my story, understanding this part is essential. We need to trust that every piece of our past and our present—the broken, the sad, the hard, just as much as the fulfilled, the good, the happy—plays a role in reaping the harvest of all that we are. That the dirt and dust is how we can know we'll bloom again.

This cadence of nature is something I've tried to mirror over the years. Beyond the garden, all around us, nature sings a song of change every ninety days. The world moves to the rhythm of the seasons: sprouting and budding and blooming and dying.

Look outside right now. No matter the time of year, you can see how much beauty wouldn't exist if not for the rise and fall of every season that came before.

For me, it's summer in Texas, which means the garden always needs watering. I was out there earlier when I noticed my dahlias are beginning to break through the soil—and I almost didn't believe it. So

I got closer, and sure enough, it looked like they'd proven me wrong. I planted them using tubers from last season's harvest, which isn't something I've done before. If you've never seen a dahlia tuber, they basically look like a clump of dry dirt. I've been growing dahlias in my garden for years, and after they bloom, I've always pulled them out and thrown them away. But last year, someone told me that those tubers can be replanted again as long as they're kept in a dry, dark place. So last summer, after the dahlias died, I pulled them all up and saved the tubers, storing them for the time in the garden shed. Honestly, I had very low expectations that they'd ever be fruitful again. Every time I walked by the crates they were sitting in, I thought to myself, *No way this works.* It turns out, those tubers that sat in the dark, neglected for nearly a year, still had all this life to give within them.

The garden holds a lot of wisdom about life. When I see its life cycle play out—growth to rest, scarcity to abundance—I can't help but look closer at the rhythms of my own life. What I've been chasing, where I've been stuck. What might grow abundantly if I was to give it more attention. Or, on the contrary, if I was to let it grow on its own. What needs to be shed to nurture something entirely new. In time, you see how our world, simply by its rotation, can become our greatest measure of when to catch and when to release, what to hold and what to let go.

If we're paying attention, sometimes we get a heads-up. Some things in life come with natural endings, just based on cultural norms we've accepted. Take my oldest son for instance. Now that he's turning eighteen, our culture says it's time for him to move on, to go to college or get a job. Because we know this natural law, Chip and I have had a chance to expect this, to plan, to prepare ourselves for it. Same goes for a lot of newness—a job, relationships, a child. We can expect there will be some growing pains. For some, these rhythms will be welcomed, because we know they are nearing. And yet even the best planners can still feel like they're being robbed of something. Perhaps there have been seasons in your own life when time seems to stretch as wide as an ocean—and then your kid says their first word or takes their first step, and suddenly they're moving out of the house. It rarely matters that you knew it was coming, that you spent weeks holding on to their hand as they learned to be brave one step at a time, and then months looking for where they'd go next as they learned to be brave in a whole new way. It's still a surprise the day it happens. The day you find yourself on the other side of that moment, and catch yourself whispering, gently, "But wait, hold on—not yet."

That's why sometimes, when I watch Drake drive away from the house, a cloud of dust trailing behind him, I'll reach for Crew's hand. Grateful that I still can.

Other moments don't allow for planning at all. Life simply chooses to catch us off guard. When it comes to the death of a loved one or an unexpected fallout of a relationship, when it comes to surprise endings, the world doesn't always play fair.

But then, we see the sun rising again. The waves rolling in again. We *can* await the beauty that grows from tragedy. The bloom that follows dust. Because it's still a rhythm—just one we don't always want to recognize.

What I'm trying to say is that some of life will be predictable, but much of it won't. Sometimes letting go will hurt, but that's how we have a frame of reference. That's how we learn to pull close the things we want to hold.

MY SISTER MIKEY is only two years younger than me, so our lives have always followed a similar cadence that made it natural to dream about building our families and our futures side by side. A year after Chip and I were married, Mikey and her new husband, David, moved in next door. And like clockwork, we both had our first kids a year apart. For a while, we shared a backyard and babysitters and meals three or four times a week. We loved making plans and never considered the other wouldn't be a part of every single one of them. We envisioned our kids running around and playing together. We imagined taking trips with our families. It came as a surprise when Mikey told me that David wanted to apply to medical school, which meant schooling and residency that would take them out of state. When Mikey left, it felt like a loss of something. Part of me, I think. She's told me that she felt a hole in her heart too.

For ten years our lives carried on. Our families grew. We saw one another two or three times a year, mostly at the births of our babies. They moved a few times for David's residency while Chip and I were growing our business. We started and ended *Fixer Upper* before Mikey moved back. It's a little sad to think of all the life we missed together during that stretch of time. But when they moved their family back to Waco, just about ten minutes down the road from us, all those dreams we'd once held started to come true. Our kids were older, but quickly became best friends. We shared meals and babysitters the same way we used to. But more than that, we also got to share in who the other grew up to be. In that absence, Mikey and I carved out identities for ourselves as wives, as mothers, as women that we'd never really been able to do when our lives were so intertwined. We got to learn about each other again in a way that felt like a gift. They've been back for five years now, but Mikey's still surprising me today. A lot of unexpected joy and closeness has come from that hole that was left in our hearts. And it's reminding me again that letting go doesn't have to be the way a story ends. There's almost always something redeeming lying in wait.

THERE'S A LOT OF COMFORT to be found in rhythm. A lot of predictability and beauty. But the nature of ebb and flow calls for a lot of disruptions too. Unexpected letting go, but also things we suddenly find ourselves holding: Surprising news, problems to solve. Spilled coffees, burned dinners. A to-do list that only grows. Things pile high so quickly, and it can block our view to all that we're trying to hold at once.

Looking back on the five years we were on *Fixer Upper,* I remember the day the show got picked up and I remember our last day of filming.

But the middle? That part is a blur. I don't fully know why. It could have been busyness, could have been distractions, could have been a temporary desire to get through it as quickly as possible. It could have been the fact that we were in shock. On one hand, we felt undeserving, and a little disoriented, and on the other, we were completely caught off guard by how wildly and quickly it was turning our lives upside down. For as fun and exhilarating and exciting as those years were, there was equal confusion, uncertainty, maybe even a little fear about the direction this would take our family. Either way, it's made me wonder if I would have done anything differently had I held those years closer. Had I fully embraced every high and every low, every bend and attempt to balance, I wonder if I'd be able to look back on that stretch of time and glean more wisdom from it.

As I look ahead at life's next turn, this time I want to know intimately what I hold in my hands. I want to choose to dwell deeply in the things I'm carrying now, letting go of what is no longer serving my life and my family in order to make space for everything that is.

NOT ALL RHYTHMS will follow a natural order. We aren't always at the mercy of time when it comes to the things we should hold and that which we need to let go. Sometimes it will be completely up to us. In those moments, I have learned to trust my soul. When we ultimately decided to take a break from *Fixer Upper*, Chip and I must have heard a hundred different rumors about why we would choose to take a step back when the show was at its peak. To many, our decision looked to be so countercultural it was difficult for them to believe that we were simply following what had been stirring in our souls—that we needed to be done, that our family needed a break. Sure, there were a lot of really good reasons it wasn't the smartest move career-wise, but we weren't listening to our brains. We were listening to that deepest chamber of our hearts, even if it didn't make complete sense to anyone else.

I'm a firm believer that the more attuned we are at the soul level—not our guts, not our minds, not even solely our hearts, but all three working in harmony—the easier it is to sense when it's time to reconsider what we're carrying. Other times it's a matter of simply listening. Not everything we want to hold wants to be held by us. It sounds a little harsh, but I've seen this play out in my own life. Certain projects I'm passionate about go nowhere for months on end, something about it not being ready or right, and until I release those expectations I'm really just running in place. I see this in plans we make for ourselves, for our families too. Even the way we show up for our children. My kids are all getting older and need me to show up for them in different ways than I've relied on for years. Rhythm can be found in parenthood too, I'm learning. And the people in our lives are usually telling us, or showing us, what they need if we're paying attention—if we're routinely asking ourselves, *What are my kids, my spouse, my friends, asking for? What are they needing?*

I've heard it said that at any given time humans are doing one of two things: they're either crying out for love or they're showing it. I take that to mean that we are simultaneously looking for something to hold and something to give away. Determining what we need but also what we have to give is kind of like finding our sweet spot—our own way of recognizing that not every season should look just one way, but a balance of highs and lows, of loss that leads to discovery, of sacrifice that pushes toward strength.

There is wisdom in knowing that if there's something we want to commit ourselves to, that often means that something else has to give. I'm not just talking about career moves. Or saying yes to opportunities. But with people, ideas and theories, lies we've told ourselves. Truths we've missed. Whatever is using up the space in our souls where it shouldn't. Whether it's taken up residence for too long or simply doesn't belong. Because now we know it's taking the place of something else. Something beautiful we want to carry instead. More than any other season of my life, I'm also learning that sometimes good things need to be let go. That the time will come when something we've carried for a while, even something we've loved holding, will need space of its own for a chance at growth.

If we can embrace the perspective this tension offers, balancing the story of each season, that's how we get to see the bigger picture. How we can shoulder a quiet confidence that reminds us that the things we hold today—whether pain or sorrow, happiness or hope—aren't meant to be carried forever. So we learn to let them matter while they're ours, and to let them go when the time is right.

And here's what I'm learning too: If I don't pay attention to what

I'm holding, if I'm not the one who chooses what I carry, I'll miss the best parts. Because the world is loud and fast, and pain can sting more than beauty; heartbreak can leave a bigger mark than joy. We tend to remember the storm more than the calm. But I know that's not an accurate picture of the life you and I are tending to.

My best advice, the thing that's working for me now, is to simply pick up what you can't or no longer want to carry forward with you, say, "Thanks for what you taught me," and let it go. Then, pick up what's still true, say, "Thanks for what you're still showing me," and hold on tight. So that even when the world forces our hand, we learn to let go on good terms. Not wasting our energy on anger or resentment or fear, even grief over what we've lost, but to spend it on joy, hope, and gratitude for what we had.

THINK ABOUT ALL THAT SITS in your own arms, be it pain, sorrow, sadness that's weighing you down—but also just the opposite: joys, freedom, a lightness today that's lifting you up. There's a good chance your life right now paints a picture of both. Just as there's a good chance you see this dichotomy at play in more corners of your world, balancing the tension between chaos on one side and still waters on the other. We are never flourishing on all fronts, yet never burning from all sides either. I think it's good we remember that.

Some of us will seek balance by trying to hold on to everything, whether we're aware of it or not. But the reality is, we can't be everywhere at once. We can't be everything to everyone. While some-times I am capable, able-bodied, and strong on multiple fronts, other times I need to step back and delegate, let go of some stuff, and really rest. Every season looks different, and each one is no less significant than the other. Not when each matters to the story you're writing.

It isn't always instantaneous, knowing what you should be letting go of or holding on to. There are the obvious ones, the things that, more than anything in your life, you care to do right by—your kids, your partner, your family, close friends, possibly even the thing you're most passionate about. But the quieter ones—the secret fears and doubts that hold you back—those I call "the silent overshadowers," and they can be harder to smoke out. It takes patience and steadiness, and we as humans tend to have a discomfort with quiet, with slow. But if life is about not what we carry but how we've held it in the end, it seems to me that even the rhythm of patience is essential—patience with sorting out what you have to let go of and what is worth holding tightly to.

We likely all have a list of things we're holding that are doing us more harm than good. Pain, guilt, regret, and self-protection seem to be part of human nature, but so is seeking revision and meaning for our lives. More than what we're afraid of, I believe, is a desire that the imprint we leave on this world would be significant, to hope that how we use the time we're given would be worthy of the opportunity. If that resonates with you, find comfort in the gracious reality that all of us get to write each and every chapter of the story our lives will tell. Despite the setbacks, despite rhythms that don't flow our way, despite the world spinning, we still get to hold every chapter, we still get a chance to write and rewrite whatever we'd like. The pen is ours, even when it doesn't feel that way.

Being a good steward of our story means trusting that how we cultivate our lives today will matter for who we become tomorrow, weaving together the old and the new, the parts of who we've been with who we are still evolving into. Some things, you'll be relieved to be rid of. Other things—the good, the beautiful—you may resist, and yet this rhythm is essential too. It's how we can paint the full picture of our lives. It's how we tell the whole story. Not just the bits and pieces that shine, but all of it—every beautiful and imperfect piece. Because this is how we can know that healing follows hurt. That joy follows sorrow. That hope follows fear. And how we can know that if we feel we're stuck in one, we're never far from the other.

I don't know what the rhythms of your life look like, but I hope that as you work to create new ones, you'll prioritize the things of life that you're longing to write about. Not just the pain, the sorrow, the misunderstandings. But also the happy, the hopeful, the tender moments that seek no attention, though you still give them yours. A story that trusts that what's on the other side of one ending is a new beginning. Because the one thing we do know is that no rhythm lasts forever. When one is disrupted, another one fills its place.

Let's choose the rhythms that move us forward, toward the flow of gratitude and hopeful expectation. Let's find strength in the way they shape us.

Letting go shows us what else our arms were made to carry.

CHAPTER SIX

Deep Roots

There's a good chance we know what matters most to us. Putting a name to these things isn't the hard part. I gather every one of us could list them out right now, the two or three or five things that, without them, life simply wouldn't feel worth living. Maybe they're the same things you've been holding as far back as you can remember. Perhaps it's something new in your life that is now hard to imagine hasn't always been there. My own list is the same one I've carried for decades: my faith, marriage, our kids, the work I believe I'm called to. I've shared already the journey it took to let go of old hurts that I'd held on to for too long, lies I needed to rewrite with truth—how, gradually, those things that held me back, I learned what it took to let them go. Cutting them loose was the only way to make room for what I wanted to hold closer. But now I'm in a season where even a few of the things I counted as sacred for the first twenty-five years of my life, the very things I fought so hard to have, to hold, are starting to feel heavy in my arms. Not because they're weighing me down, but just the opposite—they need more room to grow.

Even with our most precious things, there is ebb and flow; change comes and goes. Kids we raise grow up. Work we pour ourselves into ends, or gets too tiring, too easy, or simply needs new direction. Some relationships strengthen. Some relationships fizzle. Life is teaching me that it's not about letting go of the hard, the painful—and we have our ending. There's still change here too, even in all that's good.

You've likely heard it said that change is our only constant. Seasons come and go, and all of life changes alongside them. Everything is always in motion. Sometimes change is big and drastic and happens right before my eyes, while other times it's so slow and gradual that it goes unnoticed until I look back and see how far I've come. No matter how long it takes, nothing stays the same. For better or worse, everything is always changing.

These days, I consider myself a creature of habit. But I know something of change too. I've mentioned that my family moved a lot when I was young. My dad's work took him, and us, to a new city every few years. I learned at an early age what loss felt like. What having to walk away from friendships and homes we'd built felt like. The time we spent in one place never felt long enough. But I learned to expect change and grew to understand how it works—how at first it feels like a thief, until you learn to see it as an asset, a gift.

Every time my family arrived in a new place, we never knew how long we'd be there, and yet the idea of *temporary* never kept me from settling in, making friends, getting involved. In an odd way, knowing I could be uprooted made me try to dig roots faster. My mom was a big part of this. She knew how to create home wherever we were. She knew how to excite my sisters and me about someplace new every time, no matter what it meant leaving behind. We'd always greet every new house we moved into with the same measure of glee, running around as if it was Christmas morning, each of us calling out which room would be ours. Change was part of the life of our family, so I learned to pay less attention to that part. I was less concerned with the breaking point and the pain it would bring. I stayed focused on the moment in front of me, because somewhere, something inside me was whispering, *Hold on.*

Change can be sneaky. Sometimes, when it comes with the thrill of something new, something shiny, excitement can drown out uncertainty. It's usually in the midst of this newness that we can begin to lose our footing—the part where we have to concede to the fact that it's getting a little uncomfortable. That it's affecting us more than we thought it would, that maybe we cared more than we thought we could.

It would usually hit me the week after we'd move. All that glittered now looked rather regular in everyday light. Each time it was the same. This cycle of sadness, then excitement, anticipation, then grief. I could feel every way at once. Part of me wanting to please my parents, wanting to believe something great could be waiting on the other side of someplace new. The other part of me crying out for what I longed for most: to be deeply rooted. To find a sense of continuity and consistency, to wrap my life around something tangible—a house, a bedroom, a group of friends. With each move, I would think to myself, *Maybe this will be the one.*

It's a little ironic now to think about all those times I told myself that one day I'd be settled, that maybe I'd get married and start a family and stay in one place, and then I married Chip, who is restless by nature. Chip, whose family only ever moved once, who rarely had to feel what it was like to be the new kid. And even so, he probably loved it. Chip, who lives and dies by his sense of spontaneity. In the first ten years of our marriage, we moved ten times. *Ten.* More times than I ever did growing up. Only now, I wasn't running through each new house claiming what room would be mine. There wasn't much to thrill me about these places. They were flips, purposely chosen to be fixed up, and purposely in need of a lot of love.

At that point in our lives, Chip and I would live in the houses we were fixing up—mostly because it was the only way we could afford it. At first, I thought, *I got this.* I knew what temporary felt like. How to put down roots, then uproot, only to do it all over again. As Chip and I were buying and selling all across town, I was holding home loosely. I realized, being older and more aware of my motivations, that my sense of flexibility wasn't exactly healthy—not when I was young, and not now.

Sure, I was good at being malleable. I was getting better at going with the flow. There may have been a decade between all those moves I made with my family and then again alongside Chip—but all of it felt eerily similar. As quickly as boxes were unpacked, I could always sense the clock ticking, so I would try to get my roots fast—finding friends and decorating my room when I was a kid, and then all those years later it looked like greeting neighbors and designing our house. They were checklist items to me, and I was good at giving them all my attention. Only this time, I was realizing that my checklist had fear written all over it. I was planning my life in stretches as an act of self-preservation, a way to dim my longing for something steady.

The more houses Chip and I flipped, the more restless I became. Excitement turned to sadness, sadness to resistance—then I got mad. Mad when I had to leave something I loved, and at that point in our family, something our kids loved too. Mad that I was still, decades later, pouring so much of myself into these things that only ever slipped away from me. Sometimes, I could be pretty stubborn. Chip would tell me that the house had sold, which meant it was time to move into our next flip, but I wouldn't pack. I refused to put things into boxes until the very last minute. To tell you the truth, there were a few times when I packed up the house into trash bags instead, feeling worn out and annoyed by the symbolism of packing and unpacking boxes. There were a few occasions when you could have spotted the Gaines family driving across town by our trailer bed full of trash bags.

I couldn't see it then—the silent string of lessons I was learning in each place we called home, about how our family lived, what we needed to function well, what worked and didn't work for each of our tendencies. Every house taught me something new I might not have learned otherwise. I didn't add those up as lessons quite yet; that would come later. Instead, for the most part, I was still telling myself that every new house could be our forever home. I was so focused on that picture I'd had in my mind of what stable and steady looked like, wanting it so badly I thought I was seeing it everywhere—in every house we lived in—that I almost ignored what was actually meant for our family a few miles outside town.

When we moved to the farm, Chip and I both knew it was home. That hasn't changed in the ten years since. We've lived here the longest I've lived anywhere. When we moved in, I let my roots run deep at last, breathing it all in, relief washing over me. Finally, I was somewhere for the long haul. Even as our children and our business have grown and evolved over the years, our home has been our refuge, our stability. When we're here, I can feel the way our bones, like the wood floors, have settled over time.

Chip and I are builders by nature, but as I've reflected on the years we've been at the farm, which have felt like the busiest of our lives, it got me thinking that we all go through this phase. A stretch of time when we're in building mode. It's during these years that we find our career, maybe our spouse. Some of us go on to grow our families, we have kids, make a home, figure out our purpose. We build our lives, brick by brick, with bodies that need to be fed, bills that need to be paid. Daily prayer and weekly date nights. Monthly game days and annual holiday parties. It is in these years that we gain and add and design for ourselves a mighty landscape of things we're tending to. Arms full of a lot of goodness, hopefully of dreams fulfilled and dreams not yet realized. But also maybe children and mortgages—eighteen years to carry one, thirty to pay off the other. If you know what I mean, take a moment to pause and look around at your life. There's a lot of beauty here, in all that you've built.

That's what these past ten years at the farm have felt like. Chip and I moved into our forties here. Our kids became teenagers. Our family grew by one. Our business grew by even more. These years can feel like they bring a lifetime's worth of moments and milestones, yet move at the speed of a single season. But mostly, these are the years our roots grow really deep. When it can feel like all of life is planting and cultivating, checking on our seeds, waiting for growth, then doing it all over again. I'll be honest, I have loved every minute of it. In some ways, I feel like I was made for this side of life. To work with my hands. To create and build and help something prosper. I haven't always been great at the harvesting part, in savoring what we've sown. But I can feel it in the strength of our family, in the way we have dwelled deeply in our home.

I have the stability I craved for so long, the permanence I yearned for as a little girl and then again in the beginning years of our marriage.

I am deeply rooted in a home and family I love, in work I'm passionate about. And yet, I'm starting to feel the first rumblings of a shift in the ground beneath us.

Drake is heading off to college soon, and the dynamic of our family will change because of it. Ella has her driver's license and is driving around everywhere, already dreaming about where she'll go to college. Duke is fourteen going on twenty-five, and our free spirit, Emmie Kay, is inching closer to high school. Then there's Crew, who begins pre-kindergarten soon. Chip and I are looking out on this next half of our lives wondering how we're meant to fill the spaces our children have held. How we're meant to grow alongside them. I am sensing, also, that too much of my identity is wrapped up in our company, but I don't yet know how to hold this work I love any other way. Alongside that, I'm desiring to loosen my grip on a few qualities I've lived and died by, making me productive and efficient and successful but worn out and weary—and I'm craving instead qualities I've always reached for but could never fully grasp. Like peace, like simplicity, like presence.

Ready or not, our little corner of the world is turning, and it's made me question how I begin to uproot pieces of my life I've spent decades cultivating and nurturing. It's forced me to think differently about what it means to be deeply rooted, when all around me life is changing.

I'VE ALWAYS HEARD that back in the day farmers couldn't work the same land too many times. It needed a break from what they'd been planting to be restored back to health. The soil needed something different to yield a full harvest again. I'm starting to think our roots are much the same. Meant to grow and produce, then wither and rest, to have space to expand. That maybe even the strongest of them aren't meant to stay in one place but to grow outward, in new directions, in new ways, under different circumstances, in different hands.

For a while, the idea of being deeply rooted may have looked to me like stability. Like steadiness. Like staying in one house long enough to repaint the walls. But what I'm learning is that roots need a rhythm of their own. They need cycles of cultivation and rest. They need to taste new soil and they need to move around. They need change too, for a chance at growth.

Growth by its very nature requires change, doesn't it? I don't think we get to have one without the other. These two things are wisely and intricately woven together.

I'm realizing that when I'm rooted in the right things, change doesn't threaten growth. It catalyzes it. So that's what I'm after: a way of living that grows toward change rather than against it, that strengthens with every shift that life brings.

I still have to fight off tendencies to control the narrative. This has meant unlearning decades of being outcome-oriented, and I gather I'm not alone. Consider the way we begin a new year, thinking about the goals we want to achieve, asking ourselves where we want to be at the end of that year, at the end of five years, at the end of ten years. The last scene of a movie, the final page of a book, the finished meal on the table—we judge a lot of things by how they turn out. And through all of this, it seems we've learned to glorify the outcome of something far more than the defining moments that got us there: the spark that caught our heart's interest in the first place, times we wanted to give up but didn't, even the beauty of embracing change along the way, the courage and intent it took to stick with something we believed in. All the lessons we picked up that we might not have learned otherwise.

Maybe you're the planning type. You like to have a picture in your mind of where you want to end up, and you work your way back from it. I was that way for a while, but I found that too many distractions along the way could make me feel like I was failing every time I misstepped or was forced to reroute. I was always holding expectations, focusing on the outcome and what might come after it, forgetting that so much gets worked out during the journey. That's where the endless choices exist. The ones that determine who we are going to be and what kind of story we are going to tell with our lives. I'm learning that we can have all sorts of endings, but we also arrive there as a different version of ourselves based on the path we choose.

I THINK BACK TO TIMES I have been focused on where we might land, or how things might turn out, which in some seasons has looked like where we'd live; in others, it's the way I've imagined a family trip going, or even more recently, an intention I'd set to spend more one-on-one time with my kids.

A few years ago, we were in what felt like a very busy season, but not wanting busy to define that year with our kids, I made a commitment to what seemed like the exact opposite: an intentional night out with one kid every Thursday. In theory, a fixed date and time seemed like a good idea, but in reality, between our family's ever-changing schedule, the kids' games going into overtime, and late nights at the office, it was nearly impossible to make it happen every week. Whenever it didn't go as planned, I would feel like I was failing to keep a commitment to the very people who matter most to me. Now I can see that commitment I made to my kids more clearly for what it lacked—and it wasn't intention. My heart was in the right place. But for a while, I had placed the act above the purpose—emphasizing the outcome of that commitment as the only way to measure it.

Yet for every date night that didn't go as planned, if I could shift my perspective from what I'd envisioned as the end-all and be-all, I could more easily see the unexpected opportunities I had right in front of me—unforced and unplanned but precisely what my heart was after all along. Sometimes that looked like pulling up a chair and playing a fun card game with the kids instead of making everyone go to bed, our busy hands giving way to wandering conversation. Or noticing that the time was just right to gather everyone out on the porch, and we'd all savor the last of the light, eyes fixed on the promise of another day. Other times it looked like sneaking into the boys' room after I'd already tucked them in for the night, only to turn on their bedside lamps so we could tell just one more story—which often turned into two or three more stories. Those evenings might've looked different from what I intended, but we always found our way to one another, and that didn't have to be limited to a single day of the week.

Fixation doesn't allow for growth. It doesn't leave much margin for joy, either. Now I find myself drawn more to those unplanned moments—the ones I have to be quick to take advantage of before they pass me by. Maybe to you that sounds like the exact opposite of being deeply rooted, focusing on moments that may be fleeting. But there it is again—the outcome defining the outlook. That's the part I'm done living for. A moment of beauty, a glimpse of humor, of joy, of unexpected connection—this is where I want my soul to live.

Roots that are dependent on outcomes, on endings—the image we have in our heads of a life complete—will never grow to be anything but weeds, easily undone when the wind shifts. Because outcomes don't deepen roots—not when the in-between shows the strength of our purpose, the intricate layers of our whole story. The space between is how we have anything to write about. How we can trust there are still more chapters unwritten. I don't know how else we'd measure the fullness of who we are if not by the ways we've grown. I've come to believe that a desire to make plans that are meaningful doesn't mean they have to be unbending.

While I spent a portion of my life intent on reaching for roots that would give me stability, that would make my life predictable and steady—thinking *that* was how I'd flourish—now I'm far more interested in roots that keep me open to change.

THE WORD *intention* can feel a little loaded, maybe even a little heavy. We've talked about this idea at Magnolia in the past. One of our first issues of the magazine was dedicated to the idea of intentionality. It's something I've worked toward for a while, wanting to feel like I own my days and my time, wanting to be able to recognize my life at the end of it, having had an intimate hand in what it held. It isn't an easy thing to master, with so much to distract us. Unexpected disruptions, content overload from our culture—all these things steal from our intent. We have so much to read, to consume, to work toward every day. So much to buy, to look for, to provide. With so many options and things to plan for, it can be difficult in the day-to-day to discern what to put our minds to.

Yet, if I want to move forward believing that outcomes and ends-of-the-roads have no hold on how much I embrace this life, I have to set that intention. But I have had to do some redefining of the word. *Intention* can come across as a way to wield control. I've been down that path before, and I know it only leads to more feelings of failure. So these days, I'm looking at intention a little more freely. I'm being careful not to chain expectations to the things I want to be intentional about. For this, I'm coupling intent with delight. I want to set out with intentions that feel good and true when it comes to the way I pursue Chip and our kids, and how I approach our work at Magnolia. But now I want to leave room for more unexpected surprises within the plans I make. Giving space to that which I know I can't control. Letting that void fill with beautiful and unexpected moments that even the best planners couldn't predict.

I'm embracing change in a way I couldn't have understood as a little girl who only wanted to be firmly planted somewhere. But I will say this: all those years of moving, of learning how to hold and let go of things I loved, showed me what's left even when we move someplace new: Strength that's sown in unseen places. In our family, our values, the moments we paid better attention to knowing they'd be behind us soon. All those years I couldn't truly tether myself to places or friends, I didn't realize I was refining ideals instead—ones I'd spend the rest of my life honing and honoring. Like the importance of home, not as a place but a feeling. My willingness to embrace change even when it stings. My connection to my family, not based on circumstance but wholly in love. I forgot some of these things along the way, during those busy years of pouring myself into all that we were building.

This is why, as I move into the next chapter of my life, I am challenging myself to intentionally live for *the now*. Whatever the present looks like. Not the finish line. Not the outcome. Not thinking about how the good ol' days have passed us by or how the best is yet to come. But that right now, this very second—this is the gift. These are the days. And I'm gonna breathe them all in. I'll choose to let them matter while they're mine so I can let them go with a full heart when the time is right. And I'll do it carefully, with the kind of intention that leaves room for the inevitable winds of change.

That's another reason I love to journal. There's something about a quiet morning with my notepad and pen that opens doors and windows to the ways of my heart. I've found that time alone to be crucial to setting intentions, committing to paper how and where I want to show up that day. Being sure I am grounded in the *why* before distractions attempt to take root. Insecurities too. Sometimes I'll move things even closer, hanging notes on my bathroom mirror, in the car or the office, as reminders of what my heart truly desires.

The right intentions help us journey through times of change. Yes, I can feel myself at a significant threshold right now, but really all of life is in transition. Maybe, like me, you're nearing the halfway point. Perhaps you have kids who are starting to move out, or maybe you're just beginning, and your baby is going to be a toddler soon, and that can feel like a letting go of its own. Perhaps the job you've held for a while is one you've loved, but you can sense it's time for something new. Maybe it's something else—something you can't put a name to yet. But you can feel it, a cause for change. I think sometimes we stand at these thresholds a while before we even recognize it. I've missed a few of them myself, seasons that have come and gone without me really notic- ing. I'm grateful to sense that I'm at the gates of one now, looking out at the next half of my life. Because this time I know to check my inten- tions before I let anything go. To hold whatever I'm about to lose with gratitude rather than fear. With understanding rather than dissension.

Motherhood comes with so much change, so much shifting and rerouting as we raise up these little lives before us. I know it's futile to fight nature, so I'm trying to move with them as they reach new milestones. I know that it will be good for them to step into this next phase of life with a little less of me so there's space for a little more of who they're going to be. My heart is that my kids would rise well, trusting that they're ready to go out into the world confidently, knowing this change is good for both of us. This way it might hurt a little less when the time comes. I want to believe there can be peace and joy there because I held these changes in health.

LIVING FOR MOMENTS has completely captured my heart. I've been hell-bent on this perspective to hold each moment because I have half a lifetime's experience of seeing how quickly they go. I talk about it often with Chip, with the team at the office. I know I've already talked about it in this book, and there's a good chance I will again. But I'm willing to risk sounding like a broken record because of how deeply I believe in it. Living for moments is how we get to *feel* our lives, the nuances that far outlast circumstances, the look on faces that far outlast whatever we were focused on. I care about moments because I believe they are worthy of my attention, worthy of defining my days, months, and years. It's a promise I'm holding tightly. That's where my heart is, where my intent is: experiencing the *right now* as it unfolds.

I'm the weirdo who brings my own candle and speaker from home when we stay in a hotel, and one of the first things I'll do when we arrive is put a fresh vase of flowers somewhere in our room. This is how I mark those moments in my own way. It's how I remember the way those weekend trips smelled, how they sounded, and the way my family knew it was special. Even if we're only there for a day, I'll invest time in making our space feel like home, like we're there on purpose. Deepening our roots in the things we value. Not the flowers themselves, but the emphasis of a worthy moment so that when it's over we can remember the way it made us feel.

I guess I want a life filled with these kinds of moments because they were the ones I touched, I smelled, I embraced. I want to be deeply rooted in their presence, even if only for a month—a moment, even if only for a breath.

Because I don't want to miss it. I don't want to miss out on living my life on purpose. I don't want to miss out on having and holding and always growing.

I've made the mistake of believing that roots only grow deep in the outcome of things, whether it's a physical place, a success, a picture I held in my mind a long time ago. I've made the mistake of believing that roots do best when everything stays the same.

Right now, I can sense the shift closing in. Instead of quickly digging my feet into the place I'm standing now, instead of pulling all the familiar things of my life closer, I'm intent on letting my roots grow deeply only in places where my soul is at peace. In the moment unfolding in front of me. In the values we hold dearly. In my faith and my family. Letting whatever I hold today matter even if it's not meant to last forever. I want to hold every chapter as if it was written on purpose.

Because this, I trust, is how we look back on our days, our weeks, our years, even our lives, to say, "That's the story I meant to tell."

When I'm rooted in the right things,

change doesn't
threaten growth.
It catalyzes it.

CHAPTER SEVEN

Healthy
Things Grow

I've been spending a lot of time in my laundry room. Writing, mostly.
I brought a table and chair in here a few years ago when I realized the
place where I wash and fold may be the most sacred space in our home.
No matter what's gone on out there, how loud the world gets, I can come
back to the familiar quiet in here. The *swoosh* of the wash, the rumble
of the dryer when I've stuffed it too full, the piles undone at rest on the
floor—there's something about the ordinary, the profound absence of
performance in this space, that reminds me I am known nowhere more
than my home. This is where I journal, where I take calls; it's become

the place I go when I need to solve a problem, say a prayer, where I'll begin anything I create for Magnolia. We don't have an office at our house, but even if we did, I bet this is still where I'd burrow away. If my kids can't find me, there's a good chance I'm hanging out in the laundry room.

Do you have a place you go where it feels like a return to yourself every time you're there? A place where the stressors of the day fade away like water on stone, where you can loosen your grip on whatever you were carrying? It may be the only place in your world that welcomes empty hands. I imagine that for some, it might be the beach or the mountains, places so grand there's comfort to be found in the reminder that there's always something bigger to hold us. Maybe it's the garden, with its beauty in bloom. Or a footpath near where you live—where every crack in the pavement is a reminder you've been there before, that this place is yours. Mine is undoubtedly our laundry room. Because here, I can be all of me. Wife, child, mom, designer, cook, friend, sister, laundry folder, sure—but also *TBD*.

It's good to know I have somewhere to go when it feels like I've gone too long being seen as just one thing. The boss, the designer, the lady on TV, the decision maker. The person with all the answers. The person without any answers. It's nice to have a place to retreat when I feel that nudge to recenter, to reorient myself in only the ways that are true despite a world spinning, despite giving myself in pieces in every direction. Even if it happens to be where I fold my kids' clothes.

This notion of wanting to feel *known* is somewhat new for me. I hear how it can sound like an attempt to have a whole world of people understand who you truly are, but that's not what I'm after. I'm not so sure that's even possible. What I'm longing for is a stronger connection to who *I* believe I am. I want to know intimately what, of this life, gives me purpose, what my true passions are, and the things that make me uniquely me.

Lately, I have sensed this stirring. My soul, rising, desperate to show up more than my shadows—those fears and insecurities that keep close. I'm longing to have a seat at my own crowded table of expectations. And I can sense this stirring, also, to listen differently: less strategy, more heartbeat. To know myself a little better than I did before. To let my words and actions reflect who I am and who I believe I'm becoming—before people to my left and to my right do it for me. And maybe it sounds silly, but these days, my laundry room feels like neutral ground in the battle of who I'm growing into and who others perceive me to be. Here, I can tend to the ways I know help me grow—free of expectations and opinions from those on the outside looking in. Here, I am known. For all the ordinary, and for all the complex.

I've heard the words *seen and known* strung together before. Maybe you have too. I've always assumed they're spoken in tandem for good reason—perhaps equal in measure and weight. People talk about the value of being seen, the human desire to be known. I've used these two words interchangeably myself. But now, I'm not so sure they offer us the same thing—now that I've known what it's like to experience one, and then the other.

One comes with watchful eyes, and expectations based on glimpses. One involves performance—and perfection, if you're any-thing like me. One carries the weight of other story lines different from the one you're trying to write. The other, though, is where walls fall, where assumptions break, and where we are who we believe we are, nothing less. There's a vast distance between being seen and feeling known.

IN COLLEGE, I MAJORED in broadcast journalism with the plan of being a news anchor. I had a few misperceptions about what it would look like. I had pictured myself poised at an anchor desk, reporting on news from around the world. Sharing stories about other people making headlines, written for me by colleagues on the other side of the newsroom. I loved the idea of having a teleprompter and cue cards and a whole floor of people telling me what to do. Call it naive, but in my mind, the anchor desk was the safest place for me. There, I thought I wouldn't have to be vulnerable. I thought I wouldn't have to rely on my own wit, my own material. Not when other people would be there to tell me where to stand and what to say.

Before I ever found myself at a news desk, life surprised me with a different future, more than a few times over. And I'm better for it— people who watch the news are too. Now that I've been on those sets, and I've sat in the interview chair, the way I imagined it couldn't be further from reality. Those reporters are incredibly talented. They have to be excellent on the fly and are nowhere close to scripted or robotic. They are experts in communication and conversation. Having watched them work, I can confidently say I never could have pulled it off back then.

Yet, as flawed as my thinking was, I can't help but marvel at that grand plan I had designed for my life. Fixed at a desk, okay with thinking I would be a prop, a mouthpiece. Purposely putting myself out there in a way that only showed people a glimpse, a one-dimensional view of who I am. I was willing to be seen because by then I had mastered the art of performance, but that dream didn't allow for being known. In fact, it made sure I wouldn't have to be.

The part I'm just beginning to piece together is that my dream came true, in a way. Fast-forward a few decades, and the being seen part? That actually happened. Chip and I have found ourselves in a world where we're recognized. People know our names, our faces. Because we're not actors playing a part, those who see us have a view into our real lives. Who we are, what we do, what we're about. We've learned that fame requires that you're seen, with no guarantee that you'll ever actually be known. At least not by anyone except those closest to you—those who have a view into your life from more than just one angle. Closer than from a distance. And when I think about that, about how easy it would be for me to live out that misguided dream, it actually pierces my heart. Because now that I know my life is my story to tell, and now that I've gone back through those early chapters, sorted out who and what my heart was after, it's obvious that living out who I truly, deeply am is all I ever wanted.

It's all any of us want—to be valued for who we really are. Not to be misunderstood or misconstrued or put up on a pedestal, but known by the virtues and qualities that define us. The dreams that stir us. And not necessarily by everyone. The most intimate parts aren't meant for the masses. This isn't about trying to convince a crowded room of your true intentions. It's enough to know yourself, then to be known by those you want speaking into your life. There are a few people who know me this way these days—Chip, our children, some close friends and family. People who know that my intentions are good, that I am who I say I am—a few people whose trust I only had to earn once.

But I've lived differently. I've lived for being seen, and I've aimed to please. For a while, it felt like every part of me was in pursuit of approval, first from my parents, then my peers, then eventually, anyone who could see me. When I was a little girl, it looked like making myself small, like hiding, like only showing certain cards. As I got older, it became a more polished version of those things, still showing up as whoever people wanted me to be, only now that looked like being responsible, timely, organized. In a word: *perfect.*

And yet, people *were* seeing me. By the time I was graduating high school, I didn't feel as invisible. Those days of hiding in the library were over. I'd gotten involved in athletics—and my senior year I was homecoming queen. Being seen in those ways fueled me. I learned to live off that fleeting feeling of gratification. I learned that once we feel seen, it satisfies a human desire.

Think about a moment when you no longer felt invisible, a moment you were noticed—it can feel like a prayer answered, a *finally,* an *at last.* Years would pass before I'd understand that when we let that be enough, what usually comes next are more reasons to hide: expectations, perceptions, vying for people's approval even when what they see can only ever be skin-deep.

At twenty-one, I ended up in New York interning within the industry of my college degree because I thought that was what people expected of me. It wasn't that I had no interest in broadcast journalism—I did—but it was very obvious from day one that it was not a career suited for me.

I tend to be a rule follower. Always have. I like order. I like when things fall into place. So, when my internship ended with me realizing I didn't fit into the world of television news, I felt as though I'd just wasted four years working toward a degree that was no longer of any interest to me—not to mention all the energy and money spent along the way. I returned to Waco with no plan. I went back to working at my dad's tire shop, thinking I'd take over the business when he was ready to retire. That would make him proud, I figured. And that would make sense, I assured myself.

Something kept me from thinking outside the box I willingly lived in. Outside the degree I'd just earned, outside the family business. I was following the order of things our culture lays out for us: go to college, graduate, get an entry-level job within the industry of your degree, then work your way up. I followed the rules as we're told to, and I anchored myself to the way things are meant to go, how our culture prescribes we ought to grow. But I wasn't feeling fulfilled. I could sense that I still hadn't found the thing meant for me.

MEETING CHIP REFUTED every rule book I'd been following. He was never interested in doing things the world's way, which many might consider the right way. He was living by a manual of his own making, following his gut and betting on himself. I had never met anyone like him. I still haven't. This way of living, at first, felt completely foreign to me. I was on a huge learning curve in the early years of our marriage.

I was so sure there was a right way to grow that I nearly neglected that dream of opening Magnolia that'd been bubbling up inside of me. But the world makes it seem as though growth is linear. You get the diploma, the career, and you get promoted. As if the day after graduation we press Go and we all shuffle into line. But a one-lane highway heading in the same direction is bound to get crowded, *fast*. It wasn't easy to release the many expectations I'd shaped my life around, all the time and energy I'd invested into planning a future the way the world says we should. But Chip was challenging me to rethink what and who I was growing toward.

Perhaps you're a rule follower too. Maybe you assume, like I did, that the safest bet is to aim in one direction. That way can certainly appear surer, steadier. The irony, of course, is that this path that so many of us end up on didn't just appear on land. It was human made by hands that don't know the first thing about you.

Life alongside Chip was teaching me what it looked like to forge a path of our own. Every dream realized became a dream just beginning. The more we listened to our own hearts, and to only those who knew us best, the more convinced we were that these were the ways we were meant to go. The more we were following our own unique sense of purpose, the more purpose we found.

I'm grateful that instead of the news desk, I've found myself sitting at a different desk. Sometimes it may be tucked inside our laundry room. It may smell of a combination of baseball and yard work and lemon verbena. But here is where I can be the truest version of me, free of any expectations that aren't of my own making.

THERE WILL BE TIMES when your growth, to some, will look more like change. Like giving up or giving in. And that can unsettle people. I'll bet you can think of a few times when you've been called out or snubbed by someone for a way you've changed. A time you went about something differently or tried something new, and all people could think to say was that something must have gotten a hold on you.

That's the rub, I think. That's the reason many of us may never move beyond living for what people see. It sucks to feel like you're disappointing someone. It may even hurt you more than it hurts them to learn they think you've left them, or whatever you shared, behind.

Moments like that can make you feel like you're stuck in suspension—looking down on two versions of yourself: the one other people see and the one you're still coming into. It can be a little disorienting, and it can bring a whole lot of insecurity to the surface that makes you think twice: fears, uncertainties, even apologies.

In moments when I've felt this—like people who have seen me one way don't want me to grow, but rather want me to stay that person they think they know—I'm not offended. Most of me believes this sort of reaction isn't on purpose. I actually think the majority of us can't help but consider the sum of someone based on our relationship to them. It's easy to put people in a box of the one or two things we think they're supposed to be if it's all we've known. If they begin to evolve, that picture we have in our minds of who they are gets distorted, blurry—and change can make people uncomfortable. It's reassuring to know what's coming, that who you see is who you'll get.

I think we all do this, even if by accident. We assume the fullness of someone based on our point of view. That from where we sit, from what we see, surely it must be everything. Our kids' teachers, our doctors, our college best friends, the person we call our hero, the person we call to fix a leak. It doesn't matter how partial our view is. It doesn't matter if we're sitting in the nosebleeds. Do you think about who they are beyond who they were—or are—to you? Beyond the one or two things you've seen them do? But they have passions and families and vacations penciled into their datebooks too. They have insecurities and quiet dreams and ways they want to become better, just like you.

MY DAD JOINED OUR TEAM at Magnolia about eight years ago after working in the tire industry for nearly four decades. He was the oldest person on our leadership team by a few miles. I wanted him there because I trusted him more than anyone in the world. Magnolia was growing quickly, and we needed people by our side who had our best interests at heart. It took a few years for me to see my dad in this new light. There was the fact that he raised me, and that I know him more intimately than anyone else on our team. But he also brought with him decades of experience in an industry that's pretty uniform, where things happen one way and there's a formula to success—and we were wanting to do things differently with Magnolia.

The years we've had my dad on our team have totally surprised me. He could have walked in and laid out all his experience on the table. But instead, every day, I can tell he's showing up as a learner, willing to hear out those much younger than him. I'm watching it shape the ideas he brings to the table. I'm seeing him flourish in ways I imagine he didn't even think he could. It's a gift. Instead of feeling like he's different from the dad who raised me, I get to be proud of the man who, at seventy-three, he's still becoming.

It's the same thing with my kids. With every passing year, with every blowing out of the candles, they are each remade. They change so drastically, so regularly, that it can feel impossible to keep up with who they are in progress. There have been times when I've inadvertently placed expectations on them, ones I'd carried over from a season they'd already grown out of that were no longer serving the stage they were in.

Ones that made them think twice or make comparisons to their brothers and sisters. I'm realizing more and more, as my kids get older, even a fleeting comment that seems harmless or like an encouragement can affect them differently based on their personalities. It can affect their sense of becoming in ways I didn't intend. My words have power over my kids, and it's something I'm learning to be more mindful of.

I'll bet you can relate if you really think about it. It might be that you're known by your profession, by being called "mom" or "dad," by your relationship to someone else, by that one time you did that one thing. There are, in each of our lives, defining factors we're known by. Sometimes we get to choose them; sometimes they're chosen for us. It can happen fast, though. People see you one way and soon it's all you hear about. Expectations pile high when people think they know us. What we'll say yes or no to, how we'll react, what would be good for us, the things we should stand up for, times it would be best for us to duck or run for cover. We may push expectations toward one another and be completely unaware of it, but it does leave an impression, sometimes indelibly. Because when we find ourselves fixed in someone else's mind, it's so very easy to become fixed in our own—and if we end up living for others, for their expectations, there's no truth there. No growth either.

I've been knocked around by a lot of expectations over the years. Some of my own making, never grounded in truth. And more recently, by those of others—people who are vocal about how they believe Chip and I should use our platform. I've felt pressure to do right by people I feel seen by—and I gather I'm not alone. Perhaps you've felt that same pressure over the years. Expectations of that nature don't discriminate based on social class, race, or where you live, whether it's an audience of many or an audience of one.

I've known intimately a life of chasing expectations—no matter how many eyes are on me. I've spent seasons hustling toward something I'm not even sure I believed in. Something I would later realize wasn't ever intended for me. Sometimes the word *expectation* can cause me to shudder because of the ways I've let it weigh me down with the strength of a shadow I so badly want to step out from.

I'm still figuring out how to shield myself from expectations that don't begin within. It's a constant reorienting when it feels as though every stage of life seems to invite more in. When we go to college, when we're done with college. When we marry, enter parenthood, start or quit a job. I could go on. It's difficult to think of a phase of life that *doesn't* come with strings attached. Please don't hear that I'm against *healthy* anticipation—expectations that are grounded in hope and belief, in growth and accountability. Those are worth going for. Let's just be sure we're the ones choosing them.

In times like this, when it feels like a battle to hear your own whisper above the crowd, it's essential to go to that place where you're reminded you are more than what people see. Find your laundry room scene—a place where you can openly tend to your own growth. Where you can nurture who you are and the person you're growing into, so you can pour into the areas of your life you truly care to do right by:

your kids, your work, your relationships. It's here where all that noise fades, where you learn to nurture those quieter intentions. Once you get to a place where you can say, "This is why I'm growing"—whether it's to give your best to your family or a passion project, or simply because you're ready to bet on yourself—it becomes quite motivating to choose growth over expectations, being known over being seen.

Years ago, the idea that I'd disappointed or misled or walked away from an unmet expectation could have broken me. But these days, growth is where my heart is. Between then and now, yesterday and today, oh, how I pray I've changed.

RECENTLY, A FRIEND SAID TO ME, "If you're healthy, you're growing." At first, it seemed like an obvious observation. Of course I know that. I've tended that garden we planted in our backyard for nearly a decade. I have seen that the plants that get the water, the soil, the sun they need, are the ones that eventually break through the earth, that become anything more than just a seed. I also know that with every different type of plant, there are ways to know them better. That it's worth being curious about what will help them flourish—when best to plant and prune, at what point water and sun do more harm than good, who they'd do well to grow next to. But I've never thought to measure my own growth this way. I've never thought to ask myself, *What does healthy look like for me?*

So I did. I imagined it. I let the idea of it sink in for a day or two, and

I decided that when I am healthy it's because I know myself—deeply. For who I am, for what I need, for what, a month or year from now, I could be. When I have this sort of intimate understanding of myself it's easier for those around me—Chip, my kids, friends—to know me as well. It strengthens our connection too, when we can understand each other truthfully.

In order to flourish this way, I know there are a few things that need nurturing. But I can sense the distance between here and there. The space that exists between simply being seen and truly feeling known—full but never satisfied, growing but never thriving. I've climbed mountains to meet a world of expectations. I've run through valleys to earn the approval of people I can't even name. But it's led me here: working my way through a second chance, giving my soul a shot at the real thing.

What expectations are you living for? Think about which ones have you climbing and running and always pushing. Even with all that hustling, all that reaching, does it ever feel like you still haven't found what you're looking for?

What might happen if our reach bent inward? What if we based our lives only on what we found there: the passions, the loves, the quirks and curiosities that begin within?

And then, what if we started to live from the inside out rather than the outside in?

I'm grateful not to have reached the finish line of my life without fighting harder to be known for the things I believe define me. The partner I am to Chip, the way I nurture my children, my willingness to follow dreams even when they scare me. My desire to love people the way I believe Jesus did. The little bits and pieces that make me profoundly ordinary *and* beautifully complex.

The good news is none of us has reached the finish line. Every day, every hour, we get to decide whether we settle for being seen or let those in our world in on who we believe we were made to be.

IT'S ONE THING to rid yourself of expectations of your own making. It's another thing entirely to resist what's expected the more eyes that are on you.

When we started filming *Fixer Upper*, I was thirty-five years old. We had four kids, were renovating homes around Waco, and were also about to move into our farmhouse. I had been a designer for some time and was excited to sink my teeth into this particular project. It felt like we were going to finally put down some roots and make this home ours. It was also a style of home that I have always loved, which made the whole thing that much more enjoyable. During the first few days of demo, we discovered shiplap in nearly every space of the house. I had spotted this material before in other projects and was immediately drawn to its timeless style and the opportunity it offered to honor the original architecture of the house. The more shiplap we found, the more I knew that I wanted to expose it throughout our home. It was during and through this remodel that America was introduced to our family, so it made sense why one might sum up our design style in this very singular way, especially when it seemed as though client after client began to request a farmhouse look. But some moments since then have made me wonder how many people might still see me as that thirty-five-year-old mother of four who covers interiors in shiplap and white paint. Only now, I'm forty-four, I have five kids, and even though I love shiplap and will always enjoy the opportunity to highlight this very cool kind of history in someone's home, it's not how I would define my style. Because that's always evolving.

But this is where it gets really enticing to settle for being seen—when you feel like you've made it, like you've left your mark somewhere meaningful. You've gone and won the approval of people who are watching. You realize it's not so difficult to be those things, especially if you're good at them. So you keep showing up, you keep being who they think they see. But believe me—when we trust we've found our purpose by a particular way we're seen, that's when it becomes all too tempting to start chasing the glory of how we're perceived.

In the following years, I had a choice. I could either continue using shiplap in every project and really lean in to how people were beginning to see and define me as a designer, or I could stretch myself in new ways. The former was tempting because it felt easier, in all honesty. It's simpler to stay the same, whether we're talking about style—design or otherwise—the route you take to work, the way you parent, what you believe, and what people you listen to. Ultimately, I chose to continue evolving, and I've tried never to stop. Not just as a designer but also in the way I approach cooking and time spent in the garden. In these past few years, I've picked up painting and, most recently, beekeeping. Let me tell you, I am great at none of these things; but I am in awe of the power of reimagining what I might be drawn to as often as I need to, reaching deeper and deeper into the well of who I am to see what else might be waiting there for me.

I'm sure that I'm still fixed in some minds. Seen as the person I've been rather than as who I'm still becoming. Jo, the designer. Jo, the lady from *Fixer Upper*. The thing is, *that girl*—there are a thousand others just like her. A thousand other designers, a thousand other people whose work shows up on television. If I were to hang my hat on those two things, I wouldn't have the faintest idea about what makes me, me.

Yes, we could all do a better job of opening our minds in how we view one another. But I want to be clear on this—I don't believe that my feeling fixed is a *them* problem. It's not the problem of those who see me a certain way. It's what happens when I don't get my heart right about who and what I'm living for.

I see this playing out in our culture right now, where social media has become a prescribed formula, almost like "paint by numbers." Follow these cues, that person, him or her, post a picture just like this, and you'll catch the attention of a deeply distracted world. Share this, then that, and people will take note. Put yourself out there, perfectly posed and beautifully filtered, and you'll be seen by the masses. They sell *that* as the goal. The be-all. Eventually, we learn that social media fills none of those holes in our souls. But that's only eventually. Until then, we see one another working through how to curb that human desire to be noticed. And again, it pierces my heart just a little. Because I trust that most everyone, like me, doesn't really care to be *seen*. But sometimes the idea of really being *known* just feels too far out of reach.

I doubt we'll ever feel truly known if we're not willing to fight for the parts of us that aren't always so easily seen, if we're not honest about the fullness of who we believe we are. Because to me, being seen is fleeting. I think it's the path to living for false expectations, the path to becoming fixed, to hiding in halfness—the path to waking up one day and realizing the desk you're showing up to isn't the one intended for you.

WE ALL HAVE THIS CHOICE to be seen or known—whether a million people are watching, or just your kids, your spouse, your best friend. We can remain the person they saw ten years ago or three months ago. We can let the idea of who we've been stunt our growth. These days, I still find myself balancing that tension between evolution and expectations. Who I feel like I'm growing into bumping up against who I was to people ten years ago, one year ago, last season. The way I see me and the way you might. But this is what I'm learning: the path to growth isn't paved with perceptions.

There is such strength to knowing ourselves, to truly understanding what holds us back and then learning how to push past it. To know how we thrive, how we'll flourish if given the chance. When we can confidently find our own way, expectations lose their stronghold—the world's, other people's, even the unhealthy ones of our own making. It's this kind of reawakening that shapes our future. We relearn the things we need. We listen to the voices that know us. Truth by patient truth, we become more of who we're meant to be. And if there's one expectation we're living for, let it be this: nurture these things that let us be known. Because now we know that's how healthy things grow.

GROWTH IS
WHERE MY HEART IS.
Between
then and now,
yesterday
and today, oh,
how I pray I've
changed.

CHAPTER EIGHT

Untether

We've all dropped anchor in places: a city, a perspective, a belief, a lie we mistook as truth. Maybe you sought it out; maybe you'd say it found you. But as time wore on, comfort is what kept us tethered. And it makes sense. In a world where distractions are loud and noise is in no short supply, all that's familiar can count as sacred.

But transitions can uproot anchors. Often when we're in forward motion, what holds us back shows itself. When Chip and I were engaged, we took a trip to my hometown in Kansas so he could meet my extended family. I was excited to show him where I grew up. We drove up and down the neighborhoods where I rode my bike every day. We drove by my childhood home on Main Street, and by my elementary school, where we decided to pull in.

Together we walked up to the front entrance. All day long I'd told Chip story after story: "This is where we biked after school." "This is where my mom and my sisters and I would play tennis during the summer." I pointed out the roller rink and where my best friends had lived. I had stories to tell all across Rose Hill. Until we stood in front of the place I went to school for four years. Every familiar scene was still there. The tall gate at the entrance, the long hallways that flanked the right and left, the big oak tree we stood under waiting for the bell to ring. It hadn't changed. Not the sights, not that familiar scent of chalk and metal on the playground, warmed by the afternoon sun. I could see the kids I'd been in class with—their faces, their backpacks. I could see myself too. I swear if I'd closed my eyes, it could have been 1984.

The stories I earned here, I was not in the habit of sharing. Names I'd been called, kids who made fun of the slant of my eyes, all the ways and places I'd tried to hide. These were stories I kept buried.

But that day—Chip by my side, our new future ahead—brought out every story, every emotion, every tear with the strength of something that had been cautiously contained for too long. It was like my body was finally reacting to all those years being cramped by things to hide that it unfurled like tightly coiled rope, desperate to leave all this stuff behind.

For a while, Chip just held me. What he did next, though, started to feel like healing. He said to me, "Do you still believe what those kids said to you?" This answer I already knew, but saying it out loud right then and there became the difference between sinking and untethering.

At twenty-five I was still tangled up with these insecurities, even though I thought I'd put them behind me. I'd already done this exercise in New York a handful of years prior. I'd already rewritten these lies with truth. And yet. I think it's human nature to cling to what we've known, to tether ourselves to anchors so familiar we don't always recognize they are places we've been before.

Not all anchors are bad, of course. Some are healthy—necessary even. Anchors can keep us from floating away into places we don't want to be or drifting so off course that it's difficult to recover. The anchors of life can be significant things like faith, values, family. Or seemingly small and mundane things like cooking, reading, or running. Anchors like this can keep us safe. They guide us through uncertain seasons, help us weather a storm. Our anchors can offer us refuge in the ever-changing landscape of our lives.

But over time, they too get comfortable. You don't always notice when one or two have become old and rusty, less useful to you now than they used to be. Some anchors will begin to keep us from exploration, discovery, growth—these were likely dug into the sand beneath your feet so long ago you hardly notice they're there at all. Others were unhealthy from the start, rooted in fear, anxiety, or someone else's expectation.

The power of an anchor lies in its stronghold, in its ability to pull us back when we've edged too curiously out of range. Perhaps if you were to look around right now, you'd feel happily tethered to the anchors of your life. Maybe it's a value system, a set of beliefs, your role as partner, friend, parent. But maybe, if you look a little deeper, you might also see your-self chained to certain things that you wish you weren't—a bad habit, a frustrating part of your past that keeps resurfacing, a way of living that's doing you more harm than good. I've been anchored by the good and bad, healthy and unhealthy. Not all of them have left me reeling.

There are anchors of my life that keep me steady—my family, my faith in God, the one that pulls me closer to moments I don't want to miss, another that is grounded deeply in the truth of who I am. And there are anchors of my life that keep me hustling—my relationship with perfection, and also performance. Those were both dug into the sand a long time ago.

But this is what I know about my next twenty years: I will live them more freely.

I've said these words before over the years—to Chip, to my friends, to myself—a thousand times over. But freedom can feel like freefall. And frankly, I've never been skilled in the art of blind leaps. But in this season, in writing down my story, I am reminded that I am stronger than any anchor. Maybe not the weighty mass of steel itself, but now I have the tools to cut myself loose if I want to.

I GREW UP BELIEVING there was one way. For what, you might be wondering. Well, for everything. One way to act, one way to have faith, one way to be a good human being. However I saw something done, however I learned to do it, I considered the right way. Hopefully by now you've heard enough of my story to know it had nothing to do with overt boldness. I didn't walk around thinking I was the best by any stretch of the imagination. Simply, it was safest to believe I didn't have options. It was less risky, less vulnerable to view the world in black and white. It was easier to tell myself there was only one way; then I'd never have to wonder, I'd never have to fail.

I've always been a play-it-safe kind of girl. And I became the type of adult who still prefers sure and steady. Even today, I tend to stick to the places I feel confident and avoid things I'm less certain of. Part of this comes from how I'm wired—I'm naturally more risk averse. But it's also in the way my history has shaped me. We all grow up seeing things and hearing ideas we believe to be true—about ourselves and the world around us. Mostly because we don't know any better. So there's no reason to question it—yet. And we can't always feel our formation as it's happening. We can't always forecast what from today will go into shaping who we are tomorrow.

But time does always tell.

You caught a glimpse of my own childhood, of some things I believed too easily. While I wish I could tell you that I was refined by adversity early on, the truth is, I wouldn't walk through that fire for years. Instead, I was careful—too careful. As a little girl I'd learned from watching my mom's struggle for worthiness, then my own, that acceptance didn't come free. You had to be willing to trade the parts of yourself that might make people uncomfortable. The parts that look a little different, that don't fit into some conventional stereotype. For a while, I was willing to make that trade, not realizing that fear was the bargain. And the fear of being found out led me to fear failing. I carved out for myself a way of living that kept me in a glass box, where it felt like everyone could see my mistakes and flaws on display—and the only way to hide those was to put on a show.

I performed my way into fitting in. I learned to bury any glaring differences between myself and others. I only showed the cards people wanted or expected. Ones that looked like theirs. In my little world at the time, that looked like picking up right from wrong. It looked like steering clear of uncertain things. I didn't question what people around me were saying about who God is, what religion looks like. Performing may just be a form of hiding, but I let these things sink in. I leaned in to the ways of living around me that seemed like they were working, like they were accepted, and I held on tight.

Writing down my story has brought to my attention how heavily these anchors still weigh on me. I'm longing to be freed from a life of right and wrong, from measuring my identity based on external things. I'm aching for peaceful waters, for more of my life to look like who I am when I don't feel that pressure to perform.

Freedom has felt synonymous with truth. To live more freely, I need to cut myself loose from any ideas and beliefs that snuck into my thinking—until I can see what I've been tethered to from an honest perspective. And I want a clear view of the horizon, so if one day I'm ready to make that swim farther out to sea, there will be nothing that stops me.

These past few years, I've started to pay closer attention. I've waited for moments when one of those anchors would tug on me, and I fought like hell against that instinct to let it pull me in. If it was offering me a chance to retreat to old ways of thinking that I wanted to challenge, I'd dig in my heels until I could sort it out, until I could say, *Yes, I agree; I want you to keep ahold of me.* Or if I didn't, I'd begin the process of unraveling that particular thing. Quickly at first, and then, as I learned better, much more gradually.

I'm learning that it's the same for any of us—to fully live out who we were made to be, there is something, or several things, that each of us needs to set free.

I get that freedom is subjective. What it means to be free for one person doesn't necessarily equate to freedom for another. For some, freedom is perceived as a kind of rebellion. At times it might even look reckless. Or it can look like the opposite of reckless. It can look like taking control. I'm yearning for a little bit of all of it. I want to be rebellious toward old, unhealthy expectations. I want to recklessly pursue who I am called to be. I want to take control of how I show up for my life and the story I'm writing. Each of us may have a different perspective on how we'd define what living freely looks like. But this I know to be true: our story invites us into freedom.

OUR STREETS ARE FILLED with stories just like the ones that shaped me. Every day, we all shoulder a past that informs how we see ourselves, from our own definitions of identity and success to deep-seated notions about our worth.

Some of us see the world the way it was taught to us. Others grow up running from what was modeled for them. Either way, every day, every minute, we view the world through a lens of our own making: beliefs we pick up from uncertain or painful experiences, ways the world showed us how to perceive ourselves through its eyes instead of our own.

Think about your own life. Is there any part of it that exists because somewhere along the way someone convinced you there was no other option? A characteristic, a routine, even the career you're in or your view of family. It might be your notion of religion or politics. Really consider this: What pieces of your story are only there because someone else wrote them into it?

Perhaps it's a secondhand perception of who you are. A fleeting comment that you once took as a "note to self," but that later became part of how you saw yourself. How much of who you now see when you look in the mirror is actually made of notions from other people? Their reckless words now written into your own reflection.

Identifying these, whether they're assumed, unquestioned, or outright lies, is the first step in redeeming them. You can write them down; you can say them out loud. I have known the power that comes from speaking a truth into existence. Sometimes it's the only way to start believing it.

Maybe you, like me, have only ever known one way of thinking. Or a certain way of seeing yourself. Maybe it's all you've ever been taught, or it's all you've ever learned, and it feels comfortable, safe—it makes sense. But maybe there's a chance that at some point along the way, you bumped up against one of those long-held beliefs and you wondered, if even for a second, *But does it really make sense?* Might you actually live more freely without it? A moment that got you thinking, *Maybe there's more than one way.* While I'm an advocate for owning the whole story of your life, I don't believe that means every chapter is worthy of carrying forward—not if it's holding you back. Not if it's the reason you won't ever hold empathy and understanding in its place, or ever allow the pieces of your own brokenness to be stitched back together in ways that bring healing.

Ask yourself, *What's holding me back?* The answers can start an unraveling. You discover fear that keeps you hidden. Insecurity and shame that locks you in place. A highlight reel of false truths and unkind words that replay in your head every time you're feeling vulnerable.

There's a world of ugly hiding beneath that question, and every time I've had the courage to ask it over the last twenty years, I've caught glimpses of the shadow I'd been hiding in. Because these anchors that hold us back, they are how we talk ourselves into believing lies and out of opportunities to see things truthfully. They are what we cling to when the storm comes rolling in; they're there, we tell ourselves, to protect, to serve as shelter. As a refuge we can retreat to when we feel a threat edging closer. But once you begin to unravel, you realize that some of what you've tethered yourself to isn't even rooted in reality. They're shadows that move and morph without ever touching ground.

I think if we let them, our shadows would one day loom larger than life itself.

I've lived this way for a while. I've allowed some chapters of my past to define my present and overshadow my future. But when I imagine the life I'm reaching for now, that feels just within reach, I'm realizing that the only way I get there is by a current that moves toward truth, toward reconciliation. There's no space anymore for anchors that threaten healing.

That's why I'm untethering. It's the only way I know how to fully release something. A quick breaking free doesn't offer the same resolution as a gentle unraveling. So I'm going back through some seasons in my life where the state of things swung into focus and I was forced to take a good, hard look at how long I'd been anchored in place, and what it was that kept me bound there. A time when I was smack-dab in the middle of a moment that was a by-product of just how careful I'd been. When I could feel my body and my mind yearning to move. Somewhere, *anywhere* but there.

So that when it happens again, this time I'll listen.

I ENTERED ADULTHOOD carrying around this black-and-white way of seeing the world. I saw through this lens that convinced me there was only one way to go about living. But then I met and married Chip, who is basically a poster child for doing things not wrong or right, but some other way entirely. My narrow outlook threw us for a few loops in those early years, but it was clear that I'd brought into our marriage certain ways of thinking, of living, of managing money based on how my parents raised me. We both did. But while Chip saw them as opportunities to be refined and challenged, for a while, I hid beneath the weight of them. Not to mention that Chip and I are different in seemingly every way, except the ways that matter most to us. If his default setting is risk, mine is safety. In a matter of months, he must have blown up every plausible "right way" I thought kept the world spinning. Remember, different wasn't something I trusted. Not for a while, at least. For a while, I lived by the rules I thought people wanted and expected: polished and put together, resisting anything that would make me slip out of the version of me I was presenting.

By default, there have been times over the years when I've unintentionally put Chip into the very box I'd squeezed myself into as a little girl, the box the world can make you feel as though you need to break yourself down in order to fit into. But the more effort we put in to understanding how the other worked, the more grace there was for how we were different. Fewer expectations were exchanged. Less reshaping of the other based on our own formation. I saw, firsthand, the value of loosening my grip on a few things I'd always believed. It became clear to me that I had a choice to make. I could continue to stay anchored in place, tethered only to my version of right and wrong, thinking there was only one way to do anything, while the things I longed for most— connection, belonging, understanding—grew dimmer with distance. Or, to put it simply, I could choose to see the world in color.

I've been thinking about the place this perspective of right and wrong took root in me. It wasn't within the walls of my childhood home. My parents let me live pretty freely. They were affirming in who I was and everything I did. My dad showed me this in his steadiness. Whenever he was in the room, I felt safe and secure. Like my feet were firmly planted. My mom was the nurturer, always present. Her love was the kind you could *feel*.

The thing was, when I was being teased and excluded at school it was because of my heritage, because of the way I looked and how I was different—and I couldn't bring myself to share that pain with my mom. It was her heritage too. I didn't see the point in both of us hurting. So I shouldered it alone, and I kept it to myself. Hiding became an art. At school, I tried hiding the culture I came from. At home, I tried hiding that anything was wrong at all.

This bred an instinct to perform, to shape-shift everywhere I went. Even with my faith, I believed at an early age that God's love was conditional. I imagined that he was up in heaven grading me on every thought and every move I made, nodding his head in approval when I performed well. I became dependent on how it felt to do and be good, and then basically created a scorecard system that I handed to God at the end of every day. I was a kid still, and not yet self-aware enough to ask those around me whether these rules I'd learned to live by were actually from God. It wasn't until college that I started to see things differently because I was noticing that it was affecting my worldview—I was chafing against the idea that everything was black and white, right or wrong, and I had this nagging sense that I was missing the better picture. Of God, yes, but the world too.

I regret how deeply I let that false idea fester in me. But when a timid, rule-following little girl is given a set of religious rules and legalities, she's going to cling to those things with every inch of her. And she did, for a while. But once I began unraveling, *slowly*, that misguided view of God, the most beautiful thing I learned is that he does love me, only freely. During the season I lived in New York, I was able to truly experience the heart of God—whose kindness and grace drowns out rules, and whose love for me is unconditional. For me, God is the deepest anchor in my life. He is my constant, the way I orient everything around me.

Once I set that foundation of the truth about who God is, it sent me searching for the truth about myself too. Because if I'm being honest here, when it comes to perfection and performance, those are weights that can still pull me down.

The anchor of perfection is one you're always going to see me knee-high in the sand trying to yank out. It's another one that was dug in the ground beneath me for as long as I can remember. In some seasons, it's crippling. In others, it's led me to a deeper place of creativity. It's a vice and a gift. Sometimes both at the same time. But it's had its moments, when it's wreaked havoc on my sense of self and worthiness. It can skew the person I see when I look in the mirror, the qualities I believe I have to offer.

The only way I've known to get a handle on these anchors is by checking in every now and then. When I sense that something untrue—an idea, a belief, a way I'm seeing myself—has made itself at home in my head or in my heart, I try to quiet it with honesty. Sometimes I'll write it down; other times I'll say it in a whisper. Every now and then, I feel willed to speak it as loud as my lungs allow: "I am not who those kids said I was." "I am worthy without performing."

There have been moments when questioning aspects of my identity, religion, or my narrow sense of right and wrong have felt like a surprise airstrike on my sense of self. But a thousand other quieter instances, too, have opened my eyes to outdated ways of seeing myself. In those moments, it often takes just a gentle nudge, asking myself, *Am I anchored in truth with how I'm viewing myself? God? Others?* That's how I decide what needs releasing—what I need to be reaching for to ground me—as well as what simply needs strengthening. Sometimes ugliness rises to the surface—a few things I didn't expect. But almost always there's also something beautiful on that list, a reminder, a truth I'd forgotten was there to hold on to. I've learned to do this exercise often enough, not always with the intent of changing everything but of challenging these things I let anchor me.

THESE DIFFERENT SEASONS of unraveling have revealed a few shadows I grew up in. Shadows that wouldn't allow me the clear eyes to truly see the world around me, my place in it, and how that might look different from everyone else's. They also shielded my view of where others stand, the stories they carry too. As I've started to connect those tender dots, I've come to see just how easily this happens. How, almost naturally, we can end up shading others within our own shadows.

This isn't hard to do. We live in a culture that has made it very easy to miss one another and just keep on moving. The speed of life and the immediacy we've learned to live by has shifted the way we think, the way we interact, even the way we attempt to understand one another. More than anything, I think it's lessening how much we try to see deeply and hear genuinely from others' points of view. Think about the quickness of social media—we can approve or dismiss with a tap of a button, swipe and read only the headlines. This may be our new normal, but with how fast we're all moving, I can see why it may seem simpler, safer—more convenient—to rely on what we've always believed over what we still have to learn.

I think by now most of us have mastered the art of the sprint, so much that we sometimes forget we *can* slow down. That our gut reactions don't have to be the reactions we show. That our immediate thoughts can be softened or squelched altogether. That we can question what we believe, and that it can look different from the beliefs of our parents and even our friends. And that we don't have to have an answer for everything. Not until we've paused long enough to make sure we believe it's still true.

For me, these past few years have felt a bit like a maze, trying to navigate my way through where I stand on important issues, how much I should advocate for my opinions, what I should say and shouldn't say, who and what I should support. Maybe you can relate. It's as though opinion is the new currency of our culture—and ideas about right and wrong are expected and asked for, only to be praised or torn apart. I see the value of the collected voice, but when I look around at all the pain and hurt, the bitterness and anger that's spreading through our communities, I can't say it's opinions that we lack. We don't need more microphones on the stage or more views or judgments that aren't necessarily based on fact or knowledge, because those aren't always grounded in truth.

The best thing we can offer one another is a listening ear—a brave soul. More of us willing to step out of our own shadows to see things in a different light. Moments when we choose to lean in to hear a different perspective and let ourselves think, *Well, I've never heard it said like that before.* Moments that stretch and soften our outlook. Moments that might require the patience to learn and the resolve to persist, but also a flat-out refusal to give up on our capacity to learn, grow, and evolve. Not just for the good of ourselves. Our relationships, our kids, our work—the world—deserves the healthiest version of us.

When we're willing to uproot some of our anchors, when we're willing to say, "There might be more for me out there," I think that's where we'll find common ground between where we all stand.

To some degree, these past few years have forced many of us into this kind of unlearning. Our rhythms and routines and so much of what we relied on were disrupted by a global pandemic. It swept over us, and life as we knew it was thrown completely off-kilter. Then that same year, our eyes were opened yet again to the racial injustices that

still plague our country. With its varying levels of difficulty and dev-
astation, 2020 reminded us all of how much we don't understand, how
much we have yet to learn—about ourselves and about one another.
Because when everything changes and the world stops and we're forced
to look at ourselves, we can't help but identify what actually matters, the
bits and pieces of our lives that are worth fighting for—among so many
that need to be cut loose. And a process like this isn't always quick or
easy. For some, it can mean unlearning decades of living or thinking
a certain way.

Say we're all willing to try. It still means some discomfort. Some
slowing down. Some readiness to take stock of yourself and the world
as you see it—deciphering what's worth holding on to, gleaning what's
gold, and carrying it forward. Counting only that as sacred.

YOU DON'T OFTEN HEAR about people running *from* what they
know. It's usually the opposite. Fear of the unknown tends to unleash
the sprinter in all of us. And in a world that only seems to gain speed
and spin on things we don't understand, I can see why it may not seem
natural to question what you *do* know.

The idea of untethering can feel heavy and serious, and, in some
ways, it is a reckoning of sorts. But I've come to know a lightness to it.
How simple it can be when we're willing to be just a little bit curious.
When we're willing to cultivate a sustaining sense of interest in the
world and our place in it. When we're willing to choose a perspective

that says, beyond the pursuit of simply knowing, "There is opportunity for me to embrace things I don't know and can't yet fully understand."

A mindset like this is how we refine who we are. It's how we walk through the fire to discover the diamonds in the dust. How we begin to make repairs in the aftermath is everything—because what we rebuild matters more than whatever we broke down. This is where we remember that we are more than our histories sometimes show. There is beauty, discovery, and yes, even lightness in unexpected learning—and while curiosity is not something that comes naturally to me but is a mindset I have to intentionally pursue, I do believe it is one of the best tools we have to sharpen and grow who we are. How we know to leave behind what isn't serving us anymore, and how we know to pick up what is.

There is so much to see of this beautiful world. So much to learn, to be interested in, to uncover—and yes, to unravel—in all our corners. And we *can* still seek face-to-face. We *can* still look into each other's eyes. If this resonates with you at all, I hope you'll choose this sort of discovery: anchor to anchor, one person to another.

I want to get better at approaching each season expectant of finding things I need to release in order to make room for something more worthy. I want to make a conscious choice about what I am bringing with me and what I'm leaving behind—where I keep some of the old, the stuff that still stands, and embrace the new, the stuff that will move me forward. It means we have to slow down, push pause. But think about all there is to gain.

A practice like this is never complete, but every time I've stepped out from the shade of my own shadow, every time I've loosened the rope of an anchor, it has felt like a beautiful, breathless time-out. The old is gone and I feel made new.

I won't pretend that it's not a scary thing, releasing some of the very ideas and securities you've trusted for years to keep you from floating away. I won't pretend that releasing them means they're gone forever. These things have a way of resurfacing. Sometimes you need forgiveness to move forward. Other times it's a truth that needs to be said out loud. Every now and then, it may be that you let someone hold you while you work through it.

It's this kind of unraveling that steadies you. Even amid the sea, the waves, and the water, you're venturing more into the deep with every inch of quiet courage that's setting you free. So one day, when you hear that gentle whisper, *Untether*, you find yourself brave enough to.

This I know
to be true

our story
invites us into
freedom.

CHAPTER NINE

Piece by Piece

It may be no surprise that I love a good reveal. The resolve in a powerful story, the last scene of a movie that's had me on the edge of my seat. Punch lines, final thoughts. The finished product of hard work. I can be a rule breaker when it comes to endings. I read magazines from back to front, and almost always the final chapter of a book first. I like to visualize what's coming; I like to know what's ahead. So no judgment if you already know how this book ends—I would too.

I may have a slight discomfort with unknowns. Questions and problems unresolved, stories in suspension—all of it makes me anxious. I'm a firm believer in growth, and I'm open to change, but part of the reward in the risk to me is seeing these things get their ending.

Right now, I'm waiting out my own ending with all that I'm letting go. Once we do the brave work of releasing something we no longer want to hold—whether it's a misguided expectation, an old hang-up, a lie we accepted as truth—that moment of sincere release is euphoric; it's exhilarating. It takes a great deal of heart to be willing to untangle ourselves from certain ideas we've been tied up with for so long, and it's a vulnerable thing to be willing to trust who we could be without those things. But I hadn't thought a great deal beyond being freed. So it was unexpected what came next: lingering uncertainty about where I go from here, how hard it would be not to rush to fill my empty hands with something else, another thing I don't need. The discomfort it would bring to slowly, steadily, embrace the in-between of who I'm becoming without knowing the ending.

I WAS A CHEERLEADER in high school, and so was my little sister, Mikey. We were both on the varsity squad together. Homecoming night of my senior year, our routine was more advanced than usual. The homecoming game could always draw a larger-than-normal crowd, so we'd stepped it up a bit—more flips, more jumps, more tossing people into the air. Mikey was what we called a "flier," while I was typically in the position of "right side base." It's the job of the spotter and the two people who make up the base to toss the flier straight up, high enough for her to do a trick, then to catch her in a cradle, *gracefully*. That night, when we tossed Mikey, she skewed a little too far right, and I knew that when gravity sent her back down, it wouldn't be in our arms. Quickly, I pulled the group to the right, but ended up taking on most of Mikey's weight myself. *Not at all gracefully*. Basically, I herniated two discs in my lower back, and it's never been the same.

That was twenty-five years ago, and still, picking up something the wrong way or even a little sneeze can throw my back out for days. I get an MRI every five years, and every time the doctor offers me the same advice: exercise, get stronger, see if it's possible to strengthen other muscles that can help support the weaker areas of my back.

I've never been consistent about working out. If I picked it up, it was always with an end goal in mind, usually to be more fit or more toned. Never, ever for the sake of just being healthy. If summer was around the corner, maybe I'd exercise every day, but only for a few weeks, tops. I'm not one to hit the gym regularly. I hate running. A long walk is sometimes pushing it. The process has made me keep my distance. There's nothing quick about working out. Real results can take months, even years. Plus, I know I tend to be all in or all out, so if I were to really start exercising, I'd have to see it through. I'd have to make it a commitment, and I have plenty of those already. So every five years, I nod my head and tell the good doctor he is right, and go on living the way I always have: void of weights and running shoes.

Yet, every four to six months in the decades since, without warning, I'd find myself flat on my back for a week. I almost got comfortable with this rhythm. *It is what it is,* I'd tell myself. *Just get through it.* But it was still uncomfortable—and not just physically. It can feel like a mind game too. I don't like to sit still, especially if it's not my choice. I've spent most of my life preferring to do everything, be everything. I like to move fast. Full plate, full schedule, let's go. A week of being down like that—forced to rest—can be more painful than anything physical for someone like me. So I'd typically spend the week lying on our sofa, a little miserable, a little irritable—just biding time waiting for it to pass. Doing nothing, really, to guide myself there, to rebuild where I was weak.

It was during a particularly long episode with my back out a couple of years ago that my heart began to change in a way that I hadn't asked for. When I'm on my back, it usually means I'm stuck on the sofa in our living room. The house gets uncomfortably quiet when everyone is where they should be on a weekday: school, the office, practice.

My kids had just started a puzzle, and it sat on the table next to me. A little backstory on puzzles: they're not my favorite. All that hunting and scouring for the right piece, how disheartening it is when you think you've finally found the right fit only to realize it's a near-perfect match to the one you're looking for. When you're already holding the end in your hands—the picture is in plain sight, right there on the box. Something about my personality doesn't see the point in recreating something you're lucky enough to consider finished already. Then there's the time it takes. A five-hundred-piece puzzle can feel like the longest reveal in history. If you've ever put one together with a group, you know there's always someone at the table who is first to say, "The box must be missing this particular piece." That person is usually me.

But I had nothing better to do that day, so I started poking around at the pieces. The kids had already finished all four sides of the edge and I could tell they were starting to work their way in from each of the corners. The center was completely open, so I took to that spot first. I figured that if I could get the core sorted out, the rest might be easier to place. I worked on it nonstop over the next several days, that familiar desire to get to the reveal rising with each passing hour.

When you live for endings, the middle is a nuisance. It makes us wait. It asks us to be patient. Sometimes it requires that we try and fail and try again. When you live for resolutions, the in-between can feel like it might break you. Waiting to give someone your final answer. Waiting to hear back. Mile sixteen of whatever life marathon you're running. A change that's only just begun. Or the way I'd been feeling lately—like better was out there, but not knowing in which direction.

You see, it was around this same time that I began taking note of anchors I was tethered to. A few years ago I started to really work through specific things I wanted to begin unraveling. I had already started to loosen my grip on a few of those anchors, but I wasn't sure what I should be holding in their place—and that was making me uneasy.

Letting go is the most courageous thing I've done. In flows this rush, this unraveling. I expected freedom to follow, but what came next felt more like floating—aimlessly.

Maybe to you the idea of floating, looking out and seeing nothing but the expanse of sea—no landmarks, fewer responsibilities—sounds kind of perfect, like a deep, gorgeous exhale. Maybe the idea of empty hands sounds like freedom. Drifting makes me anxious. If I don't know where I'm going, if I don't know what's next, I might as well be lost. And when I felt like I was floating, I started reaching. For a resolution, an ending. For any clue that would steady me.

I went into fix-it mode all in the name of moving on, picking up a few new distractions along the way. And lately, I'd been sensing that familiar unrest again, that feeling I'd had from the very beginning: like I was holding on to something I shouldn't be.

My kids ended up helping me finish the puzzle. My back got better too, and by the end of the week, both behind me, I figured I'd be ready to get back to business as usual. But something about that puzzle was keeping me. I couldn't ignore the irony of what I'd seen from me that week—forcing pieces into places they don't go, glancing over at the box every few seconds to see if we were any closer to finishing the picture we were building. I'd noticed that none of the kids were looking up nearly as often as I was. They seemed content with the process, content with the slowness.

There was something here: a connection between slow and steady, anxiety and rushed endings. The latter punctuated by momentum and adrenaline, the former permitted by rest and patience and trust. My kids could leave gaps unfilled for days. They could be wrong about a piece a dozen times. I wondered why it wasn't so easy for me, why I was so quick, so intent on reaching to fill my own blank space with something. Why letting go always meant a mad dash to hold on to something else. Mostly, I wondered why it felt so contrary to my being to embrace the in-between.

I think it's human nature to fill voids, silences, gaps, missing pieces. I'm not hard on myself for wanting to hold something new in place of what I'd let go. That part, to me, seems pretty natural. I've come to believe that only when we fill that space with truth do we find lasting healing. But that was just the thing. These ideas and false beliefs I'd braved letting go of would never be healed with a quick fix. They needed time to gently unwind.

I'm grateful for a week of things I didn't ask for to show me what I needed. How essential it is to take it slow, to release the pressure, to let my eyes settle, to be wrong a few times before finding the right piece I'm meant to hold next. To ease into a place of steady among that momentum I'd lived off of for so long. I was realizing it's possible to move forward with empty hands until I could find what I was really looking for.

Building that puzzle brought my own life into focus. I'd gone about piecing myself back together the wrong way, I realized, trying to fill those open spaces before pausing to consider: What picture do I want to build here?

These past few years have been a process. I'm still working out what pieces of my life go where—the things I've worked to release, to unravel from. I'm no longer rushing resolve, no longer trying to break free completely. The space I'm occupying now is teaching me that in all these things, there's a beauty to seeking them gradually.

But slow isn't easy in a fast-paced world.

Keeping up often means being put together. I've felt like I needed to have my bearings, my wits about me, before I could move forward. I've felt like I needed to get myself right, straightened out, healthy and whole, in order to show up for others. A put-together person seems much more reliable than someone who's still figuring it out.

Maybe you've felt this way too. If you could just get the answers you need, perhaps you wouldn't feel so behind. If you could just get a couple of things sorted out, you could catch up to the life you pictured. Perhaps your identity feels too wrapped up in work or a relationship. Maybe you can't move beyond a few past hurts. Say you're ready to let go of something you no longer believe. Even when we know what we want to release, even when we see something is no longer good for us, the world keeps spinning. And most of us? We keep running.

For the sake of others, we want to heal quicker, have answers sooner. For the sake of ourselves, we want to know our purpose now, not later. It can feel like there's no time to waste another second on a path not intended for us. Some days, I feel this pressure to just ride out the waves, to just hold on tight. Because I already know that whatever is next won't wait for me to begin. It won't wait for me to get things right.

I think it may be in that precious void of unresolve, that space of unknowing—directionless but feeling like there's no time to slow—where we begin forcing pieces into places they don't go. We mend what's broken in us with temporary fixes because we're in a hurry, and good-enough will do. Over time, our lives become a series of half-hearted stitches, and that can lead to an entirely different kind of unraveling.

I can see how it's easier this way, for a time. More convenient to Band-Aid those soft spots in our souls. We learn to take the path of least resistance if we ever want to keep up. Because success, we're shown, is earned on adrenaline. It's momentum we can't afford to lose for a shot at feeling free. But what happens when our legs tire? When our anchors become too heavy again? We're back at square one. Looking for pieces to patch up this one life we've been given.

RIGHT NOW, I'M WRESTLING with my role in our business. Since 2003, Chip and I have given Magnolia every inch of us, and because it has become so intertwined with who we are, sometimes it's difficult to make out where Magnolia ends and where we begin. We're sensing this desire to make sure we're showing up in the right places. And yet, maybe unsurprisingly, the actual unraveling part has been harder than I imagined.

All these years I've thought, when Magnolia fails, I fail, and when I fail, it follows. In some ways, that reality has lessened what I'm willing to share with the world—the parts of me that want to learn what else I could grow to be, or, God forbid, the parts of me that aren't so pretty. I'm often second-guessing how my own trajectory might affect our company and every person who comes to work for us each day.

About a year ago, after feeling like I needed to release some of the responsibility I carried at the office, I made it a point to reserve a couple of days a week to be home. I was longing for more time with my family, for more time to nurture the things that fuel me outside of the work we do. It went great for a while, that initial thrill of being just a little bit freer. But slowly, as it became my new normal, it got easier to take a call during my time at home. Then, a meeting or two. Eventually, my days at home looked like a day at the office. I was also noticing that whenever I'd start to feel like something was slipping, I'd pick it back up quickly. Not fully giving myself that space I agreed to, that I'd asked for. I'm learning that when things we've tried releasing creep back in or start to go sideways, it's easy to fill what's left of that empty space the same way we used to: by holding on tight.

You don't have to lead a company to understand. Surely there are things you cling to that you fear if they were to disappear, you might too. Perhaps you feel this way when you think about dreams of your own, things you've nurtured and raised, plans you've been pushing toward your whole life. You might be afraid, if you were to let go, of what little you'd be left holding. Your relationships, your career, your image, all those shiny accolades.

Insecurities have a way of resurfacing, even when we've worked so hard to release them. There have been recent moments when a fleeting comment has left me reeling about who I think I am, when someone else's notion about who I should be has taken up too much space in my head and my heart. These moments can frustrate me because I thought

I'd learned how to dim outside expectations. I thought living for these things was behind me. I believed letting them go meant I would live more freely. Now I know these things may never fade away fully, but when I can put a name to them, and I can work out the truth, they don't linger in my thoughts as long as they used to.

Another part I didn't see coming: how strange it would feel to embrace the great quiet of a life that is carrying less. The world has taught us everything we know about abundance and scarcity. One we're taught to reach for. The other, to fear. Though lately it has felt like the world is trying to show us the value of living for less while selling us more. Contenting our human desire to slow and savor while at the same time tempting our human nature to reach and run. And honestly, between the two, most of us will choose to keep climbing the path most taken. There may be pressure in plenty, but there's also panic in lack.

We tend to accelerate when we find we're finally holding fewer things. I know I've prayed for more balance, more time, less stuff. But just as quickly, I'll find more reasons to fill my arms again. Maybe this is why it has felt like letting go is futile until I can know for sure what I am meant to hold in its place. Without a clear picture, a goal in mind, how do I know what to fight for? How do I know what to protect?

The weeks that my back has forced me to rest are always a subtle gesture of this dissonance: abundance to scarcity, full speed to a sudden stop. A reminder that healthy change needs ease; it needs time to transition.

THE OTHER DAY I had another MRI. I went to the doctor this time with a listening heart because I know I'm getting older, and I have a four-year-old who still likes to be carried—and I still want to hold him. But lately I've felt like I'm playing with fire, thinking that every time I scoop up Crew could be the time my back will betray us both.

I admitted right away that I hadn't been working out. I told him that I was ready to get serious about healing. I was desperate to be fixed, to figure out this ending. My doctor looked at me, and he told me that won't ever be the case. I'll never be void of this pain in my back. But what he said next I didn't expect: "Just rebuild where you can."

He told me that if nothing else, focus only on my core. Strengthening this part of my body could be enough to compensate for my weak back. Something about the way he said it felt like permission to rebuild gradually. Just one muscle at a time.

That permission changed everything.

Because none of us are built in a day. Strength is steady but slow. It's earned in the showing up, muscle by muscle. And also, piece by piece.

This is how I'm looking at my life now: a rebuild, not an ending.

And not from the ground up. Because we don't really get a clean slate in this life. Just as my back will never be void of this pain, I don't think our story will ever be void of these things we want to release. They are part of us, no matter how disheartening, how frustrating, how painful they may be. This isn't to say we can't learn to dim them, but to fully let go? For me, that's no longer the goal.

Only a perfectionist like myself would have blindly believed that I have to be fully healed to pursue better. So now I'm taking the pieces I have and getting stronger where I can. Looking at what I hold in my hands, for the first time curious about all the different stories those pieces could tell.

I've started working out too, which people who know me well find very entertaining. This time, not with the end in mind. This time, being okay with taking it slow. I tried to recruit a group to do it with me, bringing along my oldest sons Drake and Duke and some friends. I'm more excited about it than I have been before. I'm feeling hopeful about my back for the first time since high school. Not so overwhelmed by the idea of trying to fix it, now that I know it can be enough to get stronger where I can.

I've come to learn that stretch of space—call it the middle, the in-between, the core—is not only inevitable, it's essential. The middle is the only way we get to see things differently. It's where we get to be methodical. When it comes to your life, the rebuild is where you get to put the right pieces together in ways that feel true and good. It's where you can intentionally reorganize what you give your heart and energy to. We're all in different seasons. You might be in building mode. In the first act of life. Maybe you're like me and feel like the crescendo has passed and you're looking out on the second half. Beginning or end, or halfway through, I am learning the value of changing gears and slowing my speed.

I'm still reaching—only now for depth over distance. I can feel how it's changing me, what it's showing me. There is strength you don't know is yours until you resist the flow. And there is strength that's sown in secret when you're willing to rebuild one piece at a time.

BEAR WITH ME HERE, but as I've been thinking through this, I've actually tried to look at my life like a puzzle. But not one I'm rushing to fill. Because I am still a work in progress, and the picture of my story isn't finished yet. I have found it helpful, though, to get literal about the real estate I'm giving to each piece of my life. If you're a visual learner like me, maybe you've already started to do the same.

I see it like this: Each of our lives is made up of a bunch of pieces that fit together to make us who we are. And there are a number of emotions you might feel when you open your box and pour out its pieces: excited, overwhelmed, hopeful. Start putting a name to the pieces you see: family, children, friendships, insecurities, work, dreams, hopes, fears, mistakes, plans you've made. Maybe you, like me, still see a few pieces you've been working to release. You might uncover one that still carries a lot of pain. I don't want you to remove those completely—just push them to the side. This isn't meant to belittle what you've been through. It's to remember that it's one or two of many, and that you are the one who decides where that piece belongs.

Perhaps you can look at what you have before you with grateful eyes. I hope we all do; I hope we see all the good here, and beauty too, in the pieces we've earned. And perhaps when you look at where all those pieces sit, it feels good—it fits. Maybe there's not much that feels misplaced. Not all times, not all seasons, will we be in need of a complete rebuild.

Sometimes, it's a matter of simply reordering things. Is there something you've given too much focus? A project or relationship you want to show up more for? An insecurity that's held on for too long? For me, it's the things I want less of that I'm pushing to the edge. In their place, I'm finding more space in the center than ever before. So I'm thinking deeply about how I want to fill that most central part of me.

If you don't know where to start, that's where I'm beginning: within. Making sure my core is strong and believing that if I can get that part right, it can withstand when those things on the outskirts try to creep back in. For the first time in maybe fifteen, twenty years, I'm reordering nearly everything. Not just the painful stuff I want to release. With ambitions that Chip and I have pushed toward for so long—big dreams, fast growth, seizing opportunities—I'm sensing a desire to reconsider where those go.

We attempted a downshift once before, when we decided that season five of *Fixer Upper* would be our last. Chip and I told our colleagues, friends, and our partners at the network that we felt like we needed to slow down and take a break. We wanted to return to a sense of normalcy. Not just for the sake of our family, but our business needed us too. People who knew us well, who could see how weary we'd become, were quick to understand, but their understanding came with hesitations that slowing down would mean giving up, that it would mean losing all this momentum we had at our backs from a successful five-year run on TV.

Now, looking back, we can say pretty confidently that our core wasn't in good shape. Pieces had gotten out of whack when our lives were revolving around this one thing. I'm grateful we chose to take that step back from filming. We brought Crew into the world a little more rested, a little more like ourselves.

A year or so later, the opportunity to launch a network of our own came around. In those early conversations, I remember thinking this was way too huge. We were still catching our breaths from the last time we'd been committed to being on TV. But slowly, the opportunity turned away from focusing solely on us to this idea of sharing stories from all over the world. Incredible stories told through the lens of other people's lives. So yes, the network felt daunting, and it looked like we were returning to TV in the biggest way possible—but when the intent wasn't about Chip or me leading a bunch of shows, but about sharing these really powerful, authentic stories and shining a light on the inspiring people behind those stories, it didn't feel heavy or hard. It became an honor.

The network is a new, unexpected piece of our lives, and now a part of the company we've been carrying for the last twenty years. It's hard to believe that means this work of ours has been a priority for half of my life. It's been at the center of Chip's too, surrounded by more pieces that have come as a result: other businesses, more employees, always new dreams just beginning. I remember sitting around the table at our office seven or eight years ago when things were really starting to take off. The conversations we'd had were about chasing the impossible, moving mountains, and changing the world. It sounds a little ambitious, but we were romantics, and our dreams burned bright. They still do. I don't think we'll ever extinguish those instincts that get our hearts beating.

And yet—when I look ahead at all the changes coming for our family, this next season is calling for a shift in priorities, a shift in where we're placing our time and energy. So I'm intent on pushing a few pieces out toward the rim in order to make space to savor this last year with all seven of us under one roof.

So far, this has looked like reclaiming those few days a week at home. I'm planning for more dinners around our table on the weekends. No seismic shifts, just inches here and there. Some of those Magnolia pieces I've held close to my chest for the last seven or eight years I'm finding a place for somewhere closer to the edges. Not forever. But for now. Because in these next handful of months I want to breathe in small moments more than I want to move mountains.

That's the beauty of a rebuild: nothing has to last forever, and no change has to be drastic unless you want it to be. I'm noticing that when we're willing to reshuffle, when we're willing to listen to our instinct telling us to pick up a piece and find a better fit, we get to see the hidden magic of things in that space we're making.

On a recent Sunday, I was looking out at the week with a bit of anxiety. It was going to be a busy one for our family. I had five days of filming the cooking show ahead of me; the kids had practices and games going on. Chip and I had a lot of meetings to get through. I knew it was going to be one of those weeks I wouldn't have as much time at home as I'd like. You know how those Sunday evenings can be, when looking ahead can feel like standing at the base of a mountain, and all you can see is peak after peak.

That night, as I was trying to tuck the kids into bed, it was honestly a joke—no one was staying put. I tucked Crew in first, then went to the boys' room, and suddenly, Crew was right behind me. Then I said goodnight to Drake and Duke and walked across the hall to Emmie Kay's room. Ella was in there, and now of course, so was Crew. All of a sudden, the boys showed up too. They were messing around and cracking jokes and the girls were just laughing at their brothers. That moment lasted an hour. I was exhausted, and so was Crew, now half asleep in my arms. But I wasn't willing to be the one to call it a night. Something about that scene was soul-satisfying. Because there it was, in a moment unplanned: exactly what I want to be building.

I think about how our lives are measured—not in sweeping gestures but in moments that seek no attention. It's in the day-to-day, the places where I give the best of me, that I'm piecing together the picture I'm living.

That week ended up as hectic as I thought it would be. But that goofy Sunday night in Emmie Kay's room with all the kids ended up sustaining me. It was a beautiful reminder that sometimes it's the surprise moments that show us more of what we're meant to hold, and that a posture of thankfulness is the surest way to strengthen my core.

In a busy week that maybe doesn't look exactly like we wanted or tried to plan for, there are still unexpected moments of grace that point us toward what we were after all along. For me, these moments delight and fill me up in a way that planning it out never could.

I can't help but wonder if I would have missed the beauty of that night had I not at least been aware of the pieces I want to strengthen this season. I'm learning this isn't about strategy and planning and being overly strict with ourselves. It isn't about black-and-white lines. Just having that awareness is how I'll know to hold those moments more dearly. Experience has shown me that the best rebuilds leave a little margin for the unexpected.

WHAT ABOUT YOU? How would you rebuild the picture of your life? What is central—what piece would you put down first? Second? Maybe you resonate with how I'm feeling, like you've been building in one direction and you're ready to refocus where you put your energy. It could be that you're headed the opposite way.

My sister, Mikey, is a good example. She has been a stay-at-home mom of six for the last decade, all while holding loosely a dream of opening a plant shop. These last ten years her core has been her babies. Now they're all in school and she's found herself in a new season, one where there's a little extra space for something more. She's chasing that dream, pulling it from the edge and giving it the spotlight.

Meanwhile, my older sister, Teresa, who was also a stay-at-home mom for years, is in the middle of planning her daughter's wedding. My niece has always lived at home, so my sister is preparing to watch her daughter not only walk down the aisle but move out of the house for the first time. She is helping with the wedding plans but also quietly shifting her heart to prepare for this new territory of motherhood, knowing it will look different for the first time in twenty-two years. I've watched her transition with such joy and excitement, honor and grace. I can see that she's pursuing this change in the healthiest way.

I'm also watching longtime friends walk away from comfortable jobs to take their shot at something new. I have one friend who is turning her pain into purpose by helping others with similar hurt. My kids are trying sports teams and taking art classes to see what sparks in them.

I'm being reminded daily that the picture we're building is always changing, so long as we are—and that it's a good thing. If we'd like, the pieces we're holding could tell a thousand stories. We can rebuild our lives as often as we want. One or two pieces at a time, it's up to us.

And yet, many of us will wait a while longer. We'll push it off until things slow down. We'll wait for a better time. After we get through this tough year. Maybe once the kids' colleges are paid for we can think about rebuilding. I think there's a chance many of us hesitate to build our lives the way we want because it feels…irresponsible maybe? Too good to be true? A reality only some get to enjoy while the rest of us watch with a "sounds nice" kind of attitude?

There are endless reasons we delay. The speed at which we're all moving, for one thing. It can be hard to rebuild when we can't slow down long enough to look closely at our lives. Or maybe it's insecurity. We can let our own feelings of unworthiness and fear self-sabotage our chance at a life designed by our own two hands. I've lived that way, but I'm over that now. I'm over elevating the parts that make me look polished and feel more productive. The ones that make me more liked. More comfortable. It will be tempting to try and force pieces on ourselves that we see in other people. It will be tempting to want to feel complete. But endings don't make stories. A good story is earned in the middle, in that sacred space of becoming.

It can hurt a little to learn new things. It can hurt even more to unlearn old things. Some pieces of my story I'm pushing to the side, and others are taking center stage. But it's one of those things when once you start, once you courageously begin the process of gracious disrepair, for every one thing you release you actually find that you *can* feel a little freer. Your breathing slows and shoulders soften, showing your heart that it can too. And it all feels more sacred, more freeing the more I learn, the more I unravel, the more I gradually piece myself back together.

Do this: Consider a piece you know in your soul is right. A perfect fit. Maybe even the one that feels like it's holding everything together. Your faith, a child, a relationship, your work. Now imagine a life filled with perfect fits. I'm not trying to sprinkle fairy dust all over my point, I'm just saying I think we get more of a say than we sometimes realize. We can shuffle things around. We can rebuild when certain pieces feel out of place. We can dream and create something that's ours alone, then we can live the life we picture.

That's why I'll keep a puzzle out on the table in our living room. Why I'll watch us tend to it gradually, until piece by piece it becomes what it's meant to be. And I'll remember that the life I am building is good.

The life you are building is too. And the pieces you are holding are beautiful. Whether you let one go, whether you hold on tight, whether eventually you push some to the side, each one is a glimpse of a picture in progress. The story of how we become. We could try to find our ending. We could leave the pieces untouched. Or we can trust that among them lies a thousand more beginnings.

I want to
breathe in small
moments

more than
I want to move
mountains.

CHAPTER TEN

Have
a Fun

If you had asked six-year-old me what I wanted to be when I grew up, I would have said, with certainty, a roller skater. For some, the dream might be to teach or fight fires; for others, to write a novel or paint a masterpiece. For me, destiny looked like a future on wheels. When my sisters wanted to play house or hair salon inside, I chose my white skates with hot-pink laces every time.

On my skates, I could be anything. Fast. Bold. Curious and carefree. When I slid into them, they became an extension of myself. What memory can tell me is how it felt to be out the door and on the pavement in seconds. Skating was an inside-out sort of experience. And inside, I felt free. I felt the wind at my back, pushing. I felt the sun, the rain, anything that could catch me.

I can still see one moment so vividly. I was skating down the middle of our street, and suddenly something inspired me to start spinning—arms out, head up—round and round and round. I remember feeling in that moment a lot of things at once: joy, fun, ease. I felt bright and contagious. It was unimpeded, unencumbered, and soul-satisfying. I wasn't looking over my shoulder; I wasn't wondering if anyone might see me. It's a bit shaky of a memory, but if I close my eyes, I can picture that girl again.

Lately, I've found myself wondering: *How in the world do I get her back?*

As innocent as that moment was, as a memory, it pains me. Because it would be a long time before I would skate like that again. It was 1984, the summer I'd just turned six. I was that little girl you see on the front cover of this book. The scrape on my chin? No doubt a roller-skating injury.

We were living in Rose Hill, Kansas, and I was about to start kindergarten—which means I was only a few weeks away from carrying my jacket button to the front of the class for show-and-tell, the day insecurity introduced itself to me. I was a year or so away from learning from the kids at school how different I was from them, which led me to begin hiding certain sides of my identity. A few more years still from freezing in place whenever fear creeped in. This was before

I would learn to live for acceptance, by rules I didn't make. Before I let the world convince me it was safer to hide behind fragile walls. Before I noticed that people watch with expectations, and knowing there were eyes on me sort of changed everything.

Slowly that six-year-old me got covered up. But this was before all of that. Stripped of sentiment and emotional hindsight. Then, it was no big deal. It was just me, freely skating down our street.

Coming into my forties has brought that younger me into focus. The past handful of years has had me craving that head-up, arms-out, freewheelin' feeling. Because all those layers of pressure and expectations, all those outside forces, did pile on top of me. And they turned me into someone who, on one hand, is super responsible. I take care of things. I always have. As a school kid, I made both my sisters' lunches every night. I made my dad's lunch for work every day. I was the middle child and the peacemaker. In high school I never had a curfew because I never needed one. I was always home early. I chose to go to a college close to home, assuming I'd work for my dad after graduation. Then, when Chip and I got married and we started working together instead, I ran the books. I paid the bills. My mom has said I'm like an oak tree, steady and reliable. I think I've spent my whole life living up to that.

On the other hand, all those forces also turned me into someone who can take life too seriously. This year, writing out all these chapters of my story has shown me why I hung up my skates all those years ago. It makes sense now why I became shy. Why I became a little guarded, a little rule oriented. Reliving pages of my history has shown me how performance and perfection got ahold of my spirit. And I know that so many years of all that stuff, all that weight, have squelched certain parts of me I'm now longing for.

But it's like this: sometimes I catch glimpses of that girl I used to be. In a fit of laughter, when I'm goofy or silly or a little bit delirious. When my kids catch me dancing barefoot in the kitchen. Moments when I feel light and at ease, where I'm not worrying about whose eyes are on me. They are sacred yet fleeting reminders that there is more to me that bubbles at the surface every now and then. And I'm over reining it in. Buckling down and getting serious. Feeling uneasy and anxious anytime I let my hair down. I'm over catching glimpses and praying I'll have the willpower to make the moment last longer next time. I want a life that's brimming with unfettered delight. I want days unfurling with joy, with glee. I want more of whatever used to make my soul sing so easily.

IT DIDN'T TAKE LONG for that responsible side of me to breed fear of falling short, and in that space of wanting to do everything well, I found myself on a stage. By high school, life was a performance, and mine was a dance of exceeding expectations, avoiding failure, and never, ever letting people down.

I've shared how perfection was my safety net. I figured that if I could be everything to everyone, and portray things just so, acceptance would follow. That if I could just show the cards people wanted to see, no one would question my belonging, my worth. And so began a life of tethering myself to an idealized, unattainable version of who I am, a misty black cloud that hung over me, letting me believe that if I could just keep pace and do things perfectly, I'd feel in control. That is how I'd learn to measure feeling safe and secure—when things were perfect in my eyes.

Of course, no life is completely flaw-free. All that performing started to build a convincing story. But in real life, early in our marriage, our business was going sideways. Yet I told no one. Not my friends, not my sisters, not my parents. A few years ago, Chip and I wrote a book called *The Magnolia Story,* and we talked about those years when we were barely scraping by. When the book came out we got calls from both of our families, asking why we never said anything. Part of it had been that fear of failure, but mostly we didn't want to put that kind of burden on them.

Keeping it to myself, though, meant I dealt with it the same old way. When that area of our life felt uncontrollable, as usual, I wielded control elsewhere, trying to perfect anything I could get my hands on. First in inches, then layers, across years, then decades, that fortress I've talked about, those walls I'd put up around myself and then my family, were not only tall and sturdy but a carefully curated facade. I kept hosting dinners for our families and throwing impressive birthdays for the kids. I couldn't face failure, especially not through the eyes of my family or myself. So I hid our reality behind pretty table settings and elaborate parties.

For years, whenever we'd host a dinner or family gathering in our home, it became a rhythm for those evenings to end with me feeling completely depleted from cooking, hosting, and then stressing over how it all turned out. I never let myself indulge in the part that was meant to fill me up because I was too busy staring at the placement of the platters on the table, evaluating which ones needed fixing. I grew tired of feeling like my intentions weren't aligning. There was something in me that cared deeply about creating a space where people could feel at ease and at home within our walls, yet when the doorbell rang I suddenly started piling on expectations that everything should go perfectly.

Around this time I was learning how to design interior spaces, and people were responding to it. When the kids were young, our home was featured in a local magazine. That kind of attention made me think twice all day, every day, about how our home should appear to anyone on the outside looking in. I began to treat it the same way I imagine a museum curator might handle an exhibition of treasured artifacts. I filled it with only the most beautiful pieces I could find. I longed for it to look perfect around the clock, so I spent much of the day tidying up couch pillows and immediately picking up any messes my kids made, sometimes while they were still making them. And then one day, I looked around at this home that I had so carefully assembled and realized it didn't look anything like our family. On top of that, I had spent so much of my time cleaning up any trace of my kids that most of the rooms in our house had become places they didn't even feel comfortable in. The moment I decided to create a home that actually worked for our family, it changed me as a designer. But I have to tell you, it changed me even more profoundly as a mom and as a human being. For decades, I'd been confined and bound by these chains of performance and perfection. And the day I let my kids play—like really, truly play—those chains began to fall away. My heart stretched for how I saw myself. I finally could see that I was more than someone who could make beautiful things. I was more than someone who could give people what they wanted to see. I was also capable of creating a place that held the life of our family, and that nurtured each of us, in all our wildness, in all our quirks.

That moment unraveled the net of perfection I'd been relying on to make me feel safe and secure. I realized that I'd never felt so isolated, so alone, than when I was obsessing over making something go perfectly. And suddenly, hiding behind pretty walls seemed to be the very opposite of safe. When I learned how it felt to be held by a home that worked for our family, when I was content with making it feel like a warm respite from the outside world, to be a mom who cared more about what game the kids were playing than the mess they'd leave behind, I realized that safety feels less like control, more like love—less like performing, more like belonging.

THERE IS SOMETHING WOVEN into my very DNA—a craving for everything to reach its potential. I have learned this about myself, this appetite for helping things prosper. It's a drive I've always felt, and it runs deep, desiring a life marked by a strong sense of purpose. I want to be useful. I want to write something worth reading; I want to create something worth beholding. I don't think these are bad intentions, nor do I wish away how I'm wired. But the list goes on forever of all the ways I could be and do better in my mind. It can make me impatient and hard on myself when things fall short. High standards can easily slip into criticism, which is a space I occupy more than I care to admit. For as much as I can sit there and agree with anyone that perfect doesn't exist, inside I'm often thinking, *But we'll never know for sure unless we try.*

A lot of this goes back to vulnerability. Being willing to acknowledge that I might fall short, but I'm going to give it the very best I've got. Being okay with not meeting every expectation and reaffirming what values my identity is tied to. Even if I make a mess of things, trusting that I'm capable of making the right repairs in the aftermath.

But it's a constant regrounding.

Because haven't we all lived through a moment that shifts the earth right under our feet? The kind of moment when suddenly things are different? It might have been the moment you first noticed that your actions draw attention and invite opinion. The first time you felt uncomfortable in your own skin. It might have been a comment or a look on someone's face that made you question where you went wrong, and you never did that thing again. The year you first experienced loss—of a person, of a relationship, of confidence. For some, shifts like this are quick: you lose your footing and find a safer spot to land. For others, they provoke a gradual unsettling, and time goes by before you wake up one day not sure how you got there, or who you are anymore. And you realize you've left behind a few traits you used to treasure.

I can spot my own shift in certain scenes. My first day of kindergarten, and another first day some years later, standing frozen in place at the front doors of my high school cafeteria. Moments that shook me out of who I thought I was. I can see how those scenes, stitched together among others, slowly covered up the way I once could be.

Maybe the memory of your moment, if you can remember it, is as clear as mine. A scene that brings to mind parts of who you were that you rarely see anymore. If you've never been able to determine what made that part of you disappear, think about the first time you started to live for someone or something more than yourself. Or the reason, if you can pinpoint it, that made you quiet certain aspects of who you are. It's my experience that the two go hand in hand.

Perhaps your moment isn't rooted in your childhood. And maybe it's not perfectionism. Maybe it's an obsession with your image, or with proving yourself. A burden your parents laid on you. Maybe it's a distraction with an addiction. Whatever it may be, go back, if you can, to who you were the year, the hour, the minute before the shift happened. Is there a piece or part of that person worth reclaiming?

When I think about that question we're all asked as kids, "What do you want to be when you grow up?" I can't help but wonder what would happen if we were to ask one another as adults, "What were you like when you were young?" Who knows what pieces of our past selves might rise? Perhaps we'd see parts of who we used to be that we miss, that we might want to hold closer. But also, traits we'd forgotten were ever there to begin with.

Feeling light and at ease may not be the thing you remember. But perhaps in your younger years you were bold, or endlessly curious. Extravagant in how you loved others. Maybe you were sure of yourself, sure about what you wanted. Children, it seems, have this innate instinct to nurture the things already within them. I look at my kids now and I see they all have this pure core, a specific way about them that I didn't put there. When we're young, our bodies more easily follow our spirits. When something sparks in us, we know to chase it. Freed from a lot of adult-like things, as kids we have the space to roam and explore and be more of who we are, rarely less.

And maybe you, like me, catch glimpses of those characteristics in yourself every now and then. I don't believe we ever fully lose them. I believe they are ours as long as we have breath in our lungs. It doesn't matter how long they've been misplaced, covered up, or squelched. Because they are a part of you—a part of your story—you have not missed your chance to reclaim them.

I was recently reading about a theory called the "happiness U-curve." There was a study published a while ago that showed how happiness declines when we enter early adulthood, then rises again after middle age, taking the shape of a U. The study's findings showed that, for most Americans, our late forties bring a new sense of realism, a determination to enjoy life as it is, to enjoy ourselves as we are, and that ends up increasing happiness. What's most interesting to me is the shape of the letter itself. It's made me wonder if maybe, in more ways than one, we're destined to end up back where we begin. That perhaps I'm approaching the age where I have the life experience to sense that I'm ready to reclaim those tender first parts of me. Where growth looks like a return to some of my childhood ways. Where the healthy, grown-up version of me is arms out, head up, spinning.

This isn't to say that adulthood should be about reverting to a lifestyle of reckless abandon or being completely carefree. This doesn't mean we skirt our responsibilities. I have a full plate. We all do. We can't escape the commitments of our lives, but we can make space for a little fun too. Or curiosity, or self-care—whatever it is that you're longing for again. It's rarely the good commitments that weigh us down anyway. It's all the ones we didn't ask for, that we let seep into our heads and our hearts, that have changed us over time.

This is about acknowledging that you *can* reclaim what's already yours, what's already part of you, if you want to.

Not everyone's childhood will be worth repeating. Perhaps for some, you've spent your whole life running from who you had to be for that stretch of time. I still believe there is something in you worthy of uncovering. Something that's been disguised, hidden, waiting to see if you might set it free. Something that might make you come alive in ways you haven't experienced before. Does any part of you think there could be something more, deep down? That if you were to let it soar could fill your soul more than you know? Most of us could pretty quickly say a quality we wish we radiated more often, whether it's being more confident, kinder, more generous or courageous.

This is about believing you don't have to continue living without that thing.

I wish I would have realized this sooner in my adult life. A few specific moments come to mind that I know if I could go back and do differently, I would. One of these moments was just a few years ago.

Chip and I were included on *Time* magazine's TIME100 list—a crazy honor neither of us could really believe. We were being honored alongside some amazing people—scientists, musical influencers, political leaders, and philanthropists. It was incredible to think we'd been included on purpose. They were hosting a big party in New York City and we were invited. Chip and I are not big partygoers in general, but when we showed up at this event, it was like one of those hard-to-imagine gatherings where everyone looks like they've been there before. I'd heard there would be a red carpet, which I typically try to stay as far away from as possible. I've done something similar, and it always ends the same way—with me feeling awkward about how to stand, how to walk, what to say to reporters. I'd asked our host if there was any way we could sneak in the back, but by the time our car dropped us off, it was obvious that the red carpet was the only way in. Long story short, when we stepped onto that carpet, I totally froze. A few familiar insecurities grabbed hold of me: I told myself I didn't belong there, that I wouldn't have anything to say. My brain locked up. I'm not even sure I talked, and if I did, I don't remember anything I said. Chip was over-whelmed himself, but he did his best to get us through that first part of the night.

Thankfully, we pulled ourselves together and had a blast the rest of the evening. The whole thing felt like a dream. The dinner was deli-cious. The singers and speakers were unbelievable. It really felt like an honor to be a part of such an incredible evening.

Later that night, when Chip and I got back to the hotel, we stayed up until 3 a.m. talking through the whole event. We were in disbelief, to be honest. We still couldn't believe where we had just been. The whole night felt like an out-of-body experience. There was also a part of me wondering why I couldn't have enjoyed the *whole* night. Every moment of it. Why did walking that red carpet feel like I was standing at the doors of my high school cafeteria all over again? Afraid, again, of stepping forward vulnerably when I didn't feel like I belonged there. Especially when this time I was invited. Chip and I were being honored, yet those old fears were still able to freeze me in place.

If I could live that night over again, knowing now how deeply I want to be freed from those insecurities, I would strut down that red carpet—probably not *well*, but I'd have fun. And I'd answer the questions with a light spirit because who knows if we'd ever have that opportunity again. And what a way that would have been to remember a night we never could have imagined in the first place.

I've learned to start asking myself *why* a lot. Every day, for sure. Every hour, sometimes. I don't think we ask ourselves why enough.

Why did that moment freeze me in place? Why am I feeling vulnerable around him or her? Why does this thing matter enough to keep me up at night? Why can't I enjoy this moment? Or, if it's something that's captured our hearts—*why* is it worthy? The *why* tells you everything you need to know. How much weight this thing should carry. Whether you're in it for the right reasons. Whether it can withstand those doubts or insecurities that tend to creep in and cover up our best intentions.

I think there is value in being able to put words to these feelings, reminding ourselves there are reasons behind our hurt and our stress and our fears. That it isn't "just because." For me, insecurity and feeling like I don't belong are so ingrained in my sense of self that they aren't likely to go away completely. So, when I feel that instinct to perform, it's become essential to ask myself *why*. Is it because I'm feeling a little insecure? Am I trying to overcompensate for feeling a little out of my comfort zone? If the answer is yes, I know I'm not in it for the right reasons. I can more easily untangle myself from that bad logic when my heart and my mind can align on the why.

THIS IS WHY WE WRITE DOWN our story: To discover the gold between the lines. To have something to pull to our chests whenever we feel a stirring to sink back into the truth of who we are. To heal, yes; to love better, of course. To know what's worth fighting for. But also to have a clearer picture of how we want to spend the rest of our days. None of us knows how much more of our story we have to write. As for me, I want my next and last chapter to look like a thousand entries of a life I loved living. A life that resonates with the most precious parts of who I believe I was made to be.

If you've been writing things down as we go along, find the quality or trait or belief that you want to rise to the surface of your life. Maybe it was something from your childhood; maybe it was how you embraced your college years, or the way you showed up for the first few years of marriage or parenthood. If what comes to mind is a scene like that memory of six-year-old me on my skates, choose a word that describes the way you felt in that picture of time.

I considered this for myself last New Year's Eve. I have this tradition of choosing a word every December that I want to define the next year. Something I can hold tight to. A reminder I'll keep on my phone or write on a piece of paper I see daily. Something that will help me navigate where and how I want to show up in my life—that sort of thing. As 2021 drew to a close, I found myself in a familiar place of contemplating big, meaningful words. The kind of words that catch your attention, that sound so profound when you roll them around in your mind—words I've chosen before, like *savor, abundance, presence.*

But last December, the deeper I thought—the more I pictured that six-year-old me—the louder I could hear my mom saying, "Have a fun!" which has become her signature sign-off whenever we talk on the phone. Simple words, but weighty in truth, and made even more beautiful by her Korean accent.

My mom is such a playful person. She always has been—and she knows I tend to be an "all work, no play" kind of girl, that fun just doesn't seem to run in my blood the way it does for others. But my mom—she raised me. She knows there's more to me than that. She knows the purest parts of me, and the sides of my personality that aren't so easily shown. Like the way I could be when I'd skate down our street. That's why she reminds me every day: "Don't forget, Jojo, have a fun!"

I was just beginning to write this book, and I knew that it was going to require a lot of soul work, a lot of digging. I knew that it would all be a little overwhelming. But I was trusting that writing down my story would give me confidence, peace, and more understanding about who and what I want to live for moving forward.

As I thought about this next chapter of my life, about all that it could be, about what I wanted for myself and for our family, none of those big, meaningful words seemed to satisfy what my soul was craving. It was way simpler than that.

Less worry, more fun.

I was in the middle of my Christmas shopping at the time, and I had just ordered a pair of roller skates for both my daughters from a retro shop I'd found online. Without thinking about it too much, I logged back on and ordered a pair for myself—this time green with pink laces. Who knew if I'd ever use them—it'd been nearly four decades since I laced up—but I had just resolved to have more fun and loosen up a bit, and a pair of retro roller skates seemed like a near-perfect reminder of that.

Turns out, I do use them—*all the time.* My girls and I skate around the farm, and I love watching the surprise on their faces when they see their mom spinning out in front of the house, muscle memory proving its worth, reminding me what my heart and my mind long ago forgot.

We chase dusk down our driveway. We let the wind blow our hair back. We watch our shadows dance in the sun. Arms out, heads up— spinning round and round and round.

On my skates, I still can be anything. This past year, I've taken them just about everywhere. On days when things feel heavy or hard, I lace them up and stroll around. When I feel an urge to let loose, when I sense that I'm caring too much what people think, I reach for my skates. Every time I do, I can feel myself inching closer to my six-year-old self. I am learning to feel again those traits of mine I thought I'd lost.

The extraordinary part? It was so simple. I've spent years trying to wrangle perfection and expectations out of myself. I have prayed and journaled and sought advice from those wiser. For years I have tried to free myself from a performance mindset. And to think that a skate down my driveway is what has felt most healing.

It seems too easy, but showing up for a little more fun, giving myself over to a little more lightness, has brought the ground back beneath my feet. It has made me surer of my place in this world than I've felt in a long time. And it has led me here, writing a book more vulnerable than I ever could have imagined.

I'm relearning what it means to nurture those most precious parts of me. Some days, it feels like a fight. Fighting for the freedom to skate with my arms open and my head up. Fighting for the willpower not to care who is watching. To be someone who goes to a fancy *Time* magazine event and says the wrong thing, but I'm still laughing, I'm still having fun. Not giving fear the real estate it's had all these years. Not letting people's words or ill intentions be a reason to hold my arms close again.

But I'll do it. I'll fight to be a woman with a little girl's heart.

IT'S WORTHWHILE to have a tangible reminder of this inner rebellion. Think about what physical thing might help bring rise to this certain part of you. Could it be throwing paint on a canvas, if you want to shine a light on your creative side? What about reading in the sun, or more days spent playing, if you miss your formerly curious spirit. My skates are specific to me but a practical reminder to have more fun, and I think that can help. Perhaps there's a song that takes you back to a favorite place in time. A word or saying that stirs something in you. A person who always brings out your best. Whatever it may be, it's worth finding so you can reach for it when you need to.

Of course, this means quieting some other things. Only recently did I realize that fun, for me, is how I push back on that impulse to perform and that pursuit of perfection. Only when I abandoned control did I finally feel most free, most like myself. But a moment of fun also helps me be more present; it allows me to set intentions I feel good about.

Humor and joy and silliness dissipate fear. Believe it or not, a little bit of fun is pushing back on every one of my insecurities.

I am starting to reclaim other areas of my life where I've let my serious side recuse me from moments I now know can belong to me. I think back to the early years of my kids' childhoods. I credited my personality type as a reason to lay low. But placing my value in how responsible I could be doesn't leave much margin for play. And, as you can imagine, Chip is all fun, all the time. He's the tickler, the chaser, the Nerf gun champion—and I love watching him light up the kids' faces every day. His larger-than-life personality allowed me to stay where I was most comfortable, which, if I'm being honest here, usually meant the sidelines—waiting for Chip to tag me in once the craziness had subsided and the kids were ready to help me make dinner or cuddle on the couch.

Luckily, they're still at an age where it's cool to be silly with Mom and Dad, but I know this time in their lives won't last forever. Now, I'm jumping in sooner. No longer considering qualities like fun and playfulness to be ones that I simply didn't inherit. I don't believe that's true anymore. I *am* playful, and I have many memories that prove it. The trick is remembering I am more than my instincts sometimes show.

I think also about all the years I've spent believing I wasn't brave enough to be vulnerable. When it came to taking risks and putting myself out there, I let a picture of perfection hold me back. But this posture I'm practicing—head up and arms out—this repetition is pulling me in, closer and closer to the thrill of how it can feel to wear my heart on my sleeve. It's opening my eyes to what is even more beautiful than sharing something that's pretty and polished with the world. Instead I'm saying, "This is me, completely in progress."

Inch by inch, I'm rediscovering the girl I used to be—before the world got its hands on me. I'm getting to know parts of myself again, and it's made me sure there must be more of us out there who could use this same grace. Others who are looking to find their way back to their essential self, or looking to unearth something that has long been covered up. It might be hard to fathom for some who feel like *that* version of them is a million miles away.

Maybe it's that you want to reclaim your childhood sense of curiosity, that ease in which you could love others. Perhaps you'd give anything to feel sure of yourself like you once could. To boldly pursue what it is you want, the way you used to be able to. I am learning that feelings only take us so far. How we feel can shift like the wind. Deeper, I think, down at the soul level, we can find these things we think we've lost. But to get there, we have to do things differently. It took me shaking up my life a bit to find the parts of me I was really looking for. If you, like me, have kept those things buried for a long time, this kind of recall takes practice.

A COUPLE OF MONTHS AGO, we were set to start filming season six of my cooking show. Cooking is an anchor in my life that steadies me. My kitchen, on many days, is my favorite place to be. The cooking show is typically a good time. It's been an unexpected surprise how much I've enjoyed filming each season. But, as with many things, cooking became work, and a little less enjoyable. We were a few weeks into filming and it was starting to feel a little stagnant. I wasn't bringing much energy to the room, and it was affecting everyone. I wasn't working from my heart, and it was obvious. So the night before our last week of filming, I called the producer of the show and asked what he thought about me bringing my skates to set the next day. He loved the idea, so the next morning I threw my skates in the car. At that point, skating was really only something I did with my girls in our driveway. But I was running on empty, and I had this feeling that in order to feel differently I needed a reset. More than a nap, more than time off, more than a latte to fill me up.

Before the cameras started rolling, I laced up my skates. I figured I'd wear them as a dorky entrance to the show, then go back to business as usual. But once I saw how it changed the faces in the room, how it lightened things up, how there was a new kind of energy in the air that no one expected, I decided to keep them on for the entire show. It didn't make the day any *easier*—our set is certainly not built to double as a roller rink. There are cameras on all sides, cords everywhere. Plenty of reasons that make roller-skating a hazard. But it *was* fun. It was light, it was joyful. Anytime I was at the kitchen island and I didn't know what to say next, I'd just take a couple laps and the crew would play music. Someone thought to bring a disco ball, so we hung it from the ceiling. It ended up being the best day ever. I was out of my head and just myself. Everyone had a great time, and the show was better for it.

The best part was, at first I could tell there were some surprised faces in the room—people who thought I was far too serious to pull something like that. And in a way, it was very out of character. Yet, it was also the truest, deepest, most sacred part of me who showed up that day.

This way of living has a trickle-down effect. When you see someone living out loud, all around the room, rules break. You either jump in and follow someone's lead or you find your own corner where you thrive—whatever it is that reminds you that you have more within you than you sometimes remember.

Every time I choose fun over fear, play over performance, vulnerability over perfection, it feels like a homecoming, like I'm returning to myself after all these years.

Those are the instincts I want to nurture more than any other. Because I know that perfection is not something to rid myself of. It's forever a part of me. I'm no longer trying to release it or wrestle it out of who I am. Only now, when I can sense it creeping into spaces I don't want it to be, I have something tangible to push back with. And when I feel like things have been too serious lately, I'll know what to do.

Maybe I'll turn the music up loud and I'll sway to the beat. Maybe I'll grab my skates and go for a spin. Maybe I'll get a tattoo. I'll let loose and let myself linger. Not so quick to be pulled back in. Not so fast to be serious again. I want a life that bubbles constantly with this other side of me.

It's unlikely that I'll be all fun, all the time. But now at least I'm looking for chances. For explosions of laughter and wind in my hair. For moments of silly that turn to sweet. For waves of grace when I've done my best. For joy that washes over me. For that high of living off exactly who I was made to be. Not a care in the world except the things I care for most. I'll honor the part intrinsic to me that longs for better and best—but no longer by what I do. Instead, by who I am.

What about you? What do you want more of? Less of? We don't have to settle for a story we've fallen into. Not when we can choose to give every breath we have left to one that resounds with *Yes!* and *More!* and *That's who I was looking for!* Here's to the next chapter looking a little more like the first. Here's to writing a story that brings us back to ourselves. And for goodness' sake, let's have a fun!

fun over fear,
play over
performance,
vulnerability
over perfection,

it feels like
a homecoming.
Like I'm coming
back to myself

— AFTER ALL THESE YEARS.

CHAPTER ELEVEN

Turning the Page

Have you noticed that people always want to tell you about the book they read that was so good they couldn't put it down? It's likely because the best stories are page-turners. You know, the ones with twists and turns you didn't see coming. The characters you never thought you'd root for until you got to know them, and you just couldn't help it. It's the stories you secretly hope never end—the ones you've held too dearly to forget.

That is how I want to hold my story: dearly. I want hope tucked into every part of me. I want unexpected moments that make my heart skip a beat. I want wisdom that never fades. Where the pages in-between I secretly hope never end. Why? Because now I know there's always more to read between the lines.

I wrote this book in the order you read it. I'm not sure if it's typical to write a book this way, but it was what felt most natural to me. It was a real-time unraveling. I started writing last December. Filled with questions, but sure about the place from which I was beginning. I told you in the first chapter that I'd been looking at my life in halves. Forty-four was around the corner, and my second act was closing in. There were a handful of things I wanted to do differently this time around. I'd been working through them for a few years already—fear that was holding me back, pain that needed healing. I knew what I'd been feeling restrained by, and I could put a few words to what I thought might be missing. I also knew some of my intentions needed revising, and that I was longing to be more present, more free to give my time and energy to the things that matter most to me.

Every chapter I wrote gave way to the next. Healing led to clarity. Clarity to rebuilding. Rebuilding helped me see what I want to pull close more than anything. It took me six months to get it all down. Two years before that of scribbled notes and voice memos of thoughts and hopes and insecurities, one of the biggest among them the question of whether I'd ever have the courage to share any of it with anyone.

I've mentioned that this isn't the first time I've written down my story. But once before, when I was twenty-one and living in New York City. Then, I was writing more for healing. This time, for clarity. A part of me hoped I'd find the direction I needed to close this chapter and begin another. A buttoned-up book I could put on the shelf next to the first one I wrote all those years ago and never shared. I might have felt a little desperate, honestly. Hoping that writing it all down again would offer me answers. A few solutions, maybe, to the worn-out way I'd been feeling.

I can get a little carried away romanticizing over beginnings and endings. You know this about me: I like resolutions. It's easy for me to picture the person I imagine myself growing into. What my life could look like one day. My job and my kids' too. In some ways, I've always been drawn to this measure of life: from what was or what is to what could be.

A few years ago, when I started to feel this tug-of-war more than normal, I started to write. And the more that came tumbling out of me, the more I realized this story of mine was going to be nowhere near polished. Nowhere close to open and shut. You might not have noticed this—I didn't until we were reading the final draft—but nearly every chapter of this book is longer than the one before it. The more I was willing to peel back, the more there was of me to discover. The deeper I searched for the truth, the more of it I found.

The truth is that I was wrong to think my story couldn't still surprise me.

Because right there, in the reliving of memories I'd pushed aside, in the unfolding of moments I'd forgotten, I found more of my life than I ever thought I could capture. Beauty in places I never thought there could be. In relationships, in regrets, but also, simply, all around me. The fresh perspective I was looking for wasn't about a new way of living after all. It was about lifting my eyes and noticing, about true love and belonging. It was about vulnerability giving way to feeling worthy. Placing truth above any lies. It was about having a little more fun. And for me, it was about God, about knowing him and being loved by him in a way that anchors everything.

This book ended up revealing a reality I've always run from. The truth spilled out onto every page: my story will never be as I expect it. Not polished, not perfect, not simple. No one's is. Instead, I will always feel torn between what was or what is and what could be. I will forever exist in that space between. Life will always be a chaotic collection of pieces: dreams, wins, insecurities, hurts, profound gratitude. Too much distraction and so much beauty. I will always need to pivot and grow, and give myself over to a reckless kind of grace. Because I will never not be a work in progress.

I realized this over a conversation with my publisher. They recommended removing the phrase "I'm learning" in places throughout the book—apparently I say it *a lot*. Removing it would make me sound more sure of myself, which I don't doubt. But that's just the thing. I'm not always so sure of myself, and I *am* still learning.

This is my takeaway. The CliffsNotes version of *The Stories We Tell*: Our stories aren't meant to be historical or exist in past tense, but to live and breathe and morph and change as we do. And they aren't open and shut.

But a thousand pages turning.

Of course, there are things I still want to reach for, intentions I would like to sharpen, ways I want to live better. I've shared honestly about a few traits that still make me cringe, seasons that still pierce my heart. Some pages make me more anxious than others. But I also see my soul rising. My roots growing deeper. Parts of me I'm so proud of that no measure of change or revision or ambition can undo them. Among the deeper truths to get to and pain to work through, these pages brought me back to who I really am. The version of me I always meant to see.

In writing down my story I've gleaned more of who I'm aiming to be, but also more of who I already am. Unabridged. Through the eyes of no one else. And that space I'm making in between is what's most breathtaking. Page after page, a hundred moments to savor. Chapter after chapter, a thousand reasons to say thank you. To look up and be grounded in all that I am and all that I have *right now.*

I might have been looking for resolution, but it turns out I'd rather have a story I can't put down. I'm head-over-heels now for all those pages in between. The daily acts that seem rather regular until you look back at a lifetime of notes and memories, ramblings and recipes, lists and wishes, and see that there is nothing more sacred than a moment well-loved.

Beneath this way of living lies an undercurrent. Armed with the spirit of storytelling, every day becomes a page worth writing—even in the mundane, the dishes and the cleanup, the car rides to school and stacks of bills to be paid. Deep in our souls is where this tender know-ingness simmers:

I am building something beautiful.

Maybe not always with trumpets blaring, but in quiet melodies strung together. You are telling a story only you can. Like a bass, it reverberates with a familiar rhythm that rises and falls within every single thing. Beneath every heartbreak. Every pivot. Every triumph. Every fall. What pulls you back again is a deeper purpose:

This is my story to tell.

You can spot people who are living for something deeper. They walk out into the world differently, purposefully. What's even more appealing to me is someone living openheartedly. Someone who knows there will be highs and lows but still finds reason to celebrate every bit between. Someone who trusts they're still in progress, but worthy of love anyway.

This, I believe, is where we find one another. When we see that we're not the only ones in progress. It's in that space of working it out and looking for right fits—all the failures and wins and start-overs—that slow movement forward we all can relate to. Nothing pushes back on comparison and uncertainty like vulnerability. Like feeling that you're building something together. The in-between is where we look to our left and look to our right and see that more of us are actually on the same page than we thought. And something passes between us. An understanding, a camaraderie, a sort of heart connection: we become purpose bearers for one another.

When you can stand fully in your story, you gain this craving for more—more truth, more of others willing to share that we are proudly in progress. More breaking down of fragile walls. More person to person. The part of me that was looking for my own answers and resolutions got covered up by all the possibilities of there being other stories just like and unlike mine.

That's the extraordinary part of writing down your story. You feel like you've uncovered this secret technique to savoring life. You breathe in relief that you can finally show up fully in ways you weren't comfortable enough to before. And you have this secret you want the world to know. Because there's a certain sureness you gain as you collect the pieces of your story: yours is one of many.

We all have a story to tell. And we're not called to live that story in quiet, unknown and unseen. But we don't have to unearth and discover and heal alone. We don't have to look for endings or wait to be perfectly pieced together to start writing. There's another reality. We can share in the story our world will tell. Better yet, we can write it together.

Imagine if all the worn-out, untrue, painful chapters of our lives started to quiet, and the beautiful, unique pieces of who we are—pieces that have been covered up by the noise of a frantic world—were to rise. Imagine if the stories we tell spoke of how we loved and lost and tried our best. How we saw it all, how we felt *everything*, even the parts that hurt. How often we said, "I'm still growing, but this life I'm building is beautiful."

Imagine if the stories we tell brought us back to our truest selves.

Back to one another. Imagine if we started right now, in the midst of one ending, a new beginning.

With pencils sharp, and breaths light, we turn to a crisp page.

This time, it's your turn. What beautiful story is yours to tell?

I WILL ALWAYS ————

need to pivot and grow and give myself over to a reckless kind of grace.

Because I will never not be

A WORK IN PROGRESS.

ACKNOWLEDGMENTS

Writing this book felt like taking a chance. I knew that getting down my story would mean digging into pockets of my life and parts of who I am that I'd buried or forgotten about. I knew it would mean being vulnerable and open to surprise. It turned out to be all of those things, a hundred times over—and it wouldn't have been possible without a few people who were willing to wade into the deep with me.

Chip Carter, who showed me how to hold my story well. I'm forever grateful for this beautiful life we share.

Kaila Luna, who allowed me to talk and talk and talk while we wrote and wrote and rewrote. You listened to my thoughts and ramblings and random voice memos with patience, you wrote with understanding, and you let me process and cry and you even cried with me. Your grace through it all truly helped nurture this book into being. I could not have written it without you.

Alissa Neely, who when I told I was writing this book in secret, looked at me and said, "But we haven't finished the cookbook yet." Yet you helped me bring this book to life anyways. I am endlessly grateful for your support and your friendship.

Ella Rose Gaines, who helped me design the cover of this book. I love watching you chase after your own unique sense of creativity.

Kelsie Monsen and Whitney Kaufhold, who smiled and nodded so politely when I said I wanted to use a blurry picture of me when I was six years old for the cover. Thank you for helping design a book that means so much to me.

Our team at Harper Collins, who graciously let me wait until the very last minute to share this book. You received it with open arms and so much support.

And lastly, to every reader who made it to this final page. I truly hope you close this book believing that every piece of your story matters.

ABOUT THE AUTHOR

Joanna Gaines is the co-founder of Magnolia, a *New York Times* best-selling author, Editor in Chief of *Magnolia Journal*, and creator and co-owner of Magnolia Network.

Born in Kansas and raised in the Lone Star State, Jo graduated from Baylor University with a degree in Communications. It was an internship in New York City that prompted her desire to discover how she could create beauty for people. In a big city unknown to her, Jo always felt most at home whenever she stepped inside the cozy and thoughtfully curated boutique shops, which inspired her to open a shop of her own in Waco, Texas.

Alongside her passion for design and food, nothing inspires Jo more than time spent at home with Chip and their five kids—whether they're messing with recipes in the kitchen or planting something new in the garden.

...way of being different and the thrill of being u...

..., I was proud of who I was, and I was rea...

...nt and is unique really is the _most_ beautiful par...

...down on paper. The chapters of my life I hav...

...ng. At night I would come home and I wou...

...ly as I came to a thought I'd need to drown...

...into my chest, trailing its way across the ,

...mory I could recall - all the way back to the...

...I had tried so hard to forget. The small y...

...see if I could get close enough to feel...

...and let take root in my heart, I crossed ou...

...g, I would be weeping for that little girl,

...believing that who she was wasn't good enou...

...those painful nights - the only way to break...

...and someday would happen every time my p...

...that my soul was coming back to my body.

...knocked around and drowned out by all t...

...was came back to the surface. And what has...

...way of being different and the thrill of being u...

..., I was proud of who I was, and I was rea...

...nt and is unique really is the _most_ beautiful par...

...down on paper. The chapters of my life I hav...

...ng. At night I would come home and I wou...

...ly as I came to a thought I'd need to drown...